The Prequel to China's New Silk Road

Tilman Pradt

The Prequel to China's New Silk Road

Preparing the Ground in Central Asia

palgrave
macmillan

Tilman Pradt
Ummen Communications
Freie Universität
Berlin, Berlin, Germany

ISBN 978-981-15-4707-2 ISBN 978-981-15-4708-9 (eBook)
https://doi.org/10.1007/978-981-15-4708-9

This Palgrave Macmillan imprint is published by the registered company Springer Nature Singapore Pte Ltd.
The registered company address is: 152 Beach Road, #21-01/04 Gateway East, Singapore 189721, Singapore

To Leda

Contents

Abbreviations

ASEAN	Association of South East Asian Nations
BRI	Belt and Road Initiative
CSTO	Collective Security Treaty Organization
EAPC	Euro-Atlantic Partnership Council
ETIM	East Turkestan Islamic Movement
IMU	Islamic Movement of Uzbekistan
NATO	North Atlantic Treaty Organization
OBOR	One Belt, One Road
PfP	Partnership for Peace
PLA	People's Liberation Army
RATS	Regional Anti-Terrorist Structure
SCO	Shanghai Cooperation Organisation

CHAPTER 1

Introduction: Belt and Road Initiative

On 7 September 2013, China's President Xi Jinping delivered a speech at Kazakhstan's Nazarbayev University that bore the potential to be one of the greatest speeches of our time. This speech was titled 'Promote People-to-People Friendship and Create a Better Future' and was designed to introduce, for the first time to a public audience, the full scope of China's New Silk Road project. The details of the project, subsequently labelled the Belt and Road Initiative (BRI), were outlined later—the harbours in the sea route (the Road) and the different arms of the land route (the Belt) that would connect China and Europe. The routes of energy pipelines (for oil and gas) and a network of highways and logistic hubs have been further outlined since then. The idea and scope of this huge infrastructure project bear the potential of paramount importance not only in respect of the legacy of the Xi administration but with the possibility to alter the playground of global economics and geopolitics. This project was first made public in a speech in Kazakhstan one week before the Meeting of the Council of Heads of Member States of the Shanghai Cooperation Organisation (SCO). The timing of President Xi's speech was no coincidence. Kazakhstan, where he delivered his speech, is a key component of the land route of the 'Belt and Road Initiative' (BRI). And the Shanghai Cooperation Organisation, the multilateral organisation that brings together the member states China, Russia, Kazakhstan, Kyrgyzstan, Tajikistan, Uzbekistan, and since 2017 also India and Pakistan, is the

T. Pradt, *The Prequel to China's New Silk Road*,
https://doi.org/10.1007/978-981-15-4708-9_1

political framework to establish the required settings for a project with a dimension like that of the BRI.

Later in 2013, Xi presented his vision for the sea route of the BRI at a meeting of the Association of South East Asian Nations (ASEAN) in Jakarta, Indonesia. Again, the decision to announce the sea route in Jakarta and within the framework of an ASEAN meeting was deliberately chosen. Jakarta is an important harbour along the sea route and ASEAN is the political entity for arrangements and agreements in the South China Sea.

The Belt and Road Initiative is as much an infrastructure project as a foreign policy concept. On the one hand, it comprises concrete and visible measures—roads, railroads, power stations, bridges, and logistic hubs. On the other hand, it is a political vision for deepened (economic) cooperation and a means to increase China's access to the European Single Market—a market with a combined population of more the 500 million and a total GDP of over US$20 trillion, or US$40,000 per capita. The potential of the BRI lies in bridging the fast-growing new superpower China, an export-oriented producer of consumer goods for the wealthy European consumers, in one direction and an energy-consuming China, reliant on imports of gas and oil from the resource-rich Russia and Central Asian countries, in the other direction.

To understand the success of the BRI (so far), especially the success of the land route, the Belt, one has to understand the success of the Shanghai Cooperation Organisation (SCO). To understand the success of the SCO, one has to understand the interests and motivations of its key players.

Belt and Road: The Historic Dimension

The ancient Silk Road, the predecessor of today's Belt and Road Initiative, was a trade road between China and the West (read Rome). It was a network of trade routes mainly in Central Asia and became operational during the Han Dynasty (206–220 CE). The similarity in the location of the route and the character of the exchange (both goods and ideas) between the ancient Silk Road and the infrastructure project of our days has inspired politicians and entrepreneurs along the route.

The goods that were mainly traded in the past were silk from China and gold and silver from Rome. After the decline of the Roman Empire (the stabilising hegemon in Central Asia back then), the ancient Silk Road became unsafe and lost momentum, but it experienced a revival in the thirteenth and fourteenth centuries (and led to the famous writings of one of its travellers—the Venetian Marco Polo).

The old route started at Xi'an and stretched for 6400 kilometres through Central Asia to the Mediterranean Sea (in fact, it was rather a track for caravans of camels than a paved road) where goods were shipped further. Besides goods, ideas, techniques, and religions travelled the ancient Silk Road as well as diseases such as the Black Death pandemic in the mid-fourteenth century.

As obvious as the differences between the ancient Silk Road and the modern Belt and Road Initiative are, so are their similarities: the huge economies of China and the West are potentially complementary—an increase of trade might foster the growth of both. The exchange of ideas, techniques, culture, and cuisine might find a reciprocal benevolent reception on both sides of the trade route, spur innovation, and improve the daily life and leisure activities. This aspect should not be underrated, since the sustainable success of the BRI will not only be judged in economic terms but in respect of its image as well. The more countries and common people participate in some way and experience an advantage because of the BRI, the more political support the project will receive. The ancient Silk Road required a protector, a security provider, and after the decline of the Roman Empire, the trade along the route came to a standstill. The same applies for today's situation in parts of Central Asia—without a resilient security architecture or a powerful single protector (possibly China) the success of the Belt and Road Initiative remains questionable.

Belt and Road: The Economic Dimension

The economic potential of the Belt and Road Initiative shall not be fantasised in absolute numbers about the future amount of trade in dollars. Rather, the potential of the BRI as a game changer for the economies along its routes is interesting. According to the World Bank, the percentage of the population that lives below the defined poverty line (i.e., US$1.90 a day) is 25 per cent in Kenya, 23 per cent in Uzbekistan, and 21 per cent in Laos. If the BRI develops the economic potential of the BRI and if the planned investments are made and related infrastructure projects built, the positive spill-over effects can beneficially influence the development of economies along the route.

Especially the economies of Central Asia, which are located middle and centre of the planned Belt, expect to benefit from the increased trade along the routes. One important aspect of the BRI is the huge amount of direct (Chinese) investment in infrastructure projects in the transit countries of the BRI. The Asian Development Bank (ADP) estimates the total amount of investment required in infrastructure projects in Asia to be about US$26 trillion.[1]

This is just an estimation and only time will tell how much the various countries will actually gain from the BRI. But it is a hint at the economic potential of the BRI, looking at the effects only the preliminary work for this huge project have had on some countries. A good example for this is Russia, since the improvement of China-Russia relations was fundamental for the deepening of most political and economic relations of China with Central Asian countries.

In the mid-1990s, the trade volume between China and Russia was less than two per cent of Russia's total trade. After 2000 and as a result of the improved cooperation, especially in the sector of natural resources, the amount of trade increased significantly. Russia exported oil and gas to the thriving and energy-hungry Chinese economy, and in return, China exported manufactured goods such as clothing and telecommunication and electrical equipment to Russia. In 2018, Russia became the main supplier of oil as well as gas for China. In numbers of 2017: Russia exported goods to China worth US$39.1 billion and imported Chinese goods in the amount of US$43.8 billion, thus making China the biggest source of Russian imports (20 per cent of the total) and most important destination for Russian exports (11 per cent of the total).[2]

The increase of Chinese-Russian trade was both a facilitating means to establish trustful political cooperation and an expression of the improving political relations.

Belt and Road: The Political Dimension

Besides its potential to foster the relations between its transit countries the BRI is also a project that knots together its participants in the political dimension. The many years of preparatory work to set the stage on the political level for this infrastructure project have resulted in a substantial deepening of relations. As the next chapter will show, the political situation in the 1990s, after the collapse of the Soviet Union, was not

[1] https://www.adb.org/publications/asia-infrastructure-needs (accessed: 2020/01/30).
[2] https://oec.world/en/profile/country/rus/ (accessed: 2020/01/30).

predestined for mutually beneficial relations between China, Russia, and the Central Asian states. The 'Stans' (Kazakhstan, Uzbekistan, Tajikistan, and Kyrgyzstan) were freshly independent from the Soviet Union and eager to develop alternative relationships in the political, economic, and security (military) realms—relations alternative to Russia. Additionally, the countries were conflicted over border disputes mainly with China, and China and Russia (besides border disputes) were suspicious about the other's objectives in Central Asia. How this unfavourable situation has been improved and how the BRI was prepared on the political level is a fascinating story of recent history.

Belt and Road: The Security Dimension

Similar to the political dimension, the improvement of the security situation in Central Asia was a precondition for the realisation of the BRI as was the cooperation in the framework of this infrastructure project beneficial for the security situation in Central Asia. The unsecure borders of Central Asia in the 1990s, the unresolved border conflicts, were the first issue to be addressed before a deepening of cooperation in the political, security, and economic dimensions would have been possible. The strengthened cooperation in regard to non-traditional security threats (e.g., terrorism, trafficking, extremism) had an effect as confidence-building measures as well. The joint border controls and sharing of intelligence led to higher transparency, better understanding of the various states' security objectives, and the decrease of mistrust between Russia, China, and the Central Asian states. In the long run, the increased security situation was on various levels a precondition for the realisation of the BRI.

Belt and Road: The Stations on the Travel (Ports and Railway Hubs)

The Belt and Road Initiative consists, fundamentally, of a land route and a sea route. The sea route (labelled the '21st Century Maritime Silk Road' or the Road) connects the harbours on China's east coast with Europe. The sea route spans through the South China Sea and the Indian Ocean, and passes the Suez Canal to the Mediterranean Sea. Along this sea route exist a number of strategically important harbours (and additional harbours are planned) to support trade and to link economies and markets.

The important harbours (coined 'String of Pearls' in several publications) are Jakarta in Indonesia, Hambantota in Sri Lanka (under construction), Malé on the Maldives (under construction), Gwadar in Pakistan, and Mombasa in Kenya (under construction), and the ports of Piraeus in Greece and Venetia in Italy (somehow a reminiscence to the ancient Silk Road traveller Marco Polo). There exists an alternative sea route, heading from China's east coast harbours to the north, passing Russia's northern coast and via the Arctic Ocean connecting with Europe. This northern route is often referred to as the 'Polar Silk Road' but it lacks the number of supportive harbours and is inferior in regard to the economic opportunities compared to the aforementioned sea route via the South China Sea and Indian Ocean.

Nonetheless, the Polar Silk Road possesses a strategic value given the unstable political situation in the South China Sea (due to unresolved territorial claims) and the potential of a blockade of the Malacca Strait (also known as China's 'Malacca Dilemma').

In this book, the prequel for the realisation of the land route of the BRI through Central Asia is told since this part of the BRI is already a reality. Additionally, the story of how the many obstacles in the political and security realms to realise BRI have been overcome in Central Asia is enlightening and is an explanation for China's optimism in respect of the future development of the BRI.

The current routes in overview:

'China's Belt and Road Initiative'—The Sankei Shimbun/JAPAN Forward (2018)

The land route (labelled as the 'Silk Road Economic Belt' or the 'Belt') connects China via Kazakhstan, Russia, Belarus, and Poland with Germany and Western Europe. The railroad connects China's harbour cities (e.g., Shanghai) with Chongqing to Urumqi in China's western Xinjiang region. Important logistic hubs on the route to Europe are Astana (Kazakhstan), Kasan and Moscow (Russia), Minsk (Belarus), and Warsaw (Poland) before the train reaches its destination in Duisburg (Germany). There exists an additional southern railway route of the Belt, with a turn at Urumqi to Tashkent (Uzbekistan) and via Tehran (Iran), Istanbul (Turkey), Sofia (Bulgaria), and Budapest (Hungary) to Germany. But this railway route is in large parts yet to be constructed and given the unstable security situation in various areas of this route and the number of transit countries, the northern railway route (which is already operational) is the realistic Belt.

At this moment, the Belt, as well as the Belt and Road Initiative in general, is a developing vision, a political strategy with infrastructural and economic components. Only the future will tell to what degree the great plan will be realised and how many of the various possible routes on land and at sea will become operational. The BRI possesses great potential but also faces serious obstacles. First of all, the realisation of this geopolitically major project depends on the continued economic strength and political will of the main driver behind it—China. The potential in the economic as well as political realm of this project is paramount but speculations about the future terms of trade and so on have been discussed enough. This book is about the current state of the Belt and its prequel. It analyses the ground-laying work, China's efforts in the 1990s and 2000s that opened doors and prepared the ground for the developments we are now witnessing.

Belt and Road: The Prequel

On 31 August 2012, a new railroad connection called YuXinOu was officially put into operation. The Chongqing-Xinjiang-Europe International Railway crosses 11,179 kilometres from its origin in the Chinese city of Chongqing to its destination in Duisburg, Germany. The train passes through China, Kazakhstan, Russia, Belarus, and Poland before arriving in Germany. The journey takes on average 16 days for the distance and is thus 20 days lesser than a ship would need from China's eastern coast to Germany. Time is money. The World Bank has developed a formula to figure the tradeoff between saving money and saving time: each day's delay of goods from the factory to the consumer is estimated to reduce trade by one per cent.

On its inauguration, the railway was coined the 'modern Silk Road' because it revived the ancient land route of merchants between Europe and Asia. It is noteworthy that this railway became operational almost exactly a year before President Xi introduced his vision of a New Silk Road in his speech at Kazakhstan in September 2013. The prophecy overtakes itself.

The dimension of the Belt and Road Initiative is far bigger than a single railway connection between a station in Germany and one in Chongqing. And yet the jury is out about the realisation and success of the important project envisaged by the Chinese leadership. However, the progress reached so far, the operational railway connection between Germany and China activated in 2012 and the further implementation of infrastructure work following Xi's speech of 2013 are already realtity—the groundwork and preconditions for this project to materialise have been laid in the late

1990s and early 2000s. The diplomatic efforts to improve the political relations in Central Asia, the security cooperation programmes to pacify the areas of the BRI, and the economic programmes to win the several state actors for the BRI were essential prerequisites for the BRI to develop as it does.

* * *

Bibliography

Ghiasy, Richard/Su, Fei/Saalman, Lora. 2018. The 21st Century Maritime Silk Road. Stockholm: SIPRI

Pradt, Tilman. 2016. China's New Foreign Policy. London: Palgrave Macmillan

CHAPTER 2

The Setting: Geopolitical Situation in the 1990s and 2000s

The 1990s was a period of substantial change, globally. For Europe, Asia, and Central Asia, this time was especially characterised by the dissolution of the Soviet Union and the respective impacts of this geopolitical shock for the political, economic, and security realms.

Together with the first years of the new millennium (the 2000s), this time span, 1989–2012, was the time in which the required preconditions for the Belt and Road Initiative (BRI) had been established (the setting). These roughly 20 years represent a phase of extreme geopolitical impact since all major actors on the international stage (i.e., US, Russia, China, EU) were in a phase of substantial transition (politically and/or economic) and had to handle important security issues.

This setting of transition, of challenges and opportunities, made the period of 1989–2012 a rare window of opportunity for state actors to improve their position in the international system. The weakness of one actor or alliance was the chance for others to fill the power vacuum.

China

For China's Belt and Road Initiative, the substantial changes in political, economic, and security situations in Central Asia have been an opportunity to win partners. But China was itself in a difficult situation back then. The suppression of demonstrations on Tian'anmen Square in 1989 was

T. Pradt, *The Prequel to China's New Silk Road*,
https://doi.org/10.1007/978-981-15-4708-9_2

followed by an international isolation of China—with potentially severe repercussions for China's economic development.

As a direct consequence of the Tian'anmen Square protests, Jiang Zemin became General Secretary of the Communist Party of China (as successor of Zhao Ziyang, who had sympathies for the student protests) in 1989. Subsequently, Jiang became President of the People's Republic of China (PRC) in March 1993 and stayed in office for ten years (until March 2003). The years 1995–1996 were the pivotal years of his administration.

In 1995, the visit of Taiwan's (Republic of China) then President Lee Teng-hui to the United States and his public speech at Cornell University was assessed by Chinese policymakers a step too far towards a Taiwanese independence. Jiang (who was also Chairman of the Central Military Commission from 1990 to 2005) opted for a show of force and China's army (the People's Liberation Army–PLA) conducted missile tests off the Taiwanese shore a month after President Lee's visit to the US. The Chinese missile tests were followed by military exercises in the Taiwan Strait. As a reaction, and to show support for Taiwan, the US had sent in March 1996 two carrier battle groups to the vicinity of Taiwan (in 1979, the Taiwan Relations Act (TRA) came into power, enacted by the US Congress; while not a security guarantee for Taiwan's sovereignty, the TRA is a statement that the US will support Taiwan to be able to determine its future by only peaceful means).

PLA responded to the presence of the two US carrier battle groups in the Taiwan Strait by conducting military exercises involving 150,000 troops. The situation, coined as 'Taiwan Strait Crisis', did not result in military conflicts but deepened the political isolation in international affairs China was confronted with in the aftermath of Tian'anmen in 1989. Additionally, the show of force of the US Navy off China's coast, which was clearly superior to China's navy (PLAN) and air force (PLAAF) with regard to modern weapon systems, demonstrated to China's policymakers the limitations of its power-projection capabilities westwards (Pradt 2016).

In the same year, 1996, another crucial development regarding China's foreign policy took place. In April 1996, the Shanghai Five grouping was established, comprising the heads of state of China, Russia, Kazakhstan, Kyrgyzstan, and Tajikistan. The Shanghai Five was a club created to strengthen military trust in the border regions, and was the predecessor of the Shanghai Cooperation Organisation (SCO).

The next paramount leader's period, Hu Jintao was General Secretary of the Communist Party of China from 2002 to 2012 and President of the People's Republic of China from 2003 to 2013, was hugely affected by the next geopolitical shock, namely the terrorist attacks of 9/11. When on 11 September 2001 the terrorist group Al Qaeda, in coordinated attacks, hit the US, the former setting of friends and foes on the international level experienced a reset. The airplane attacks in New York (World Trade Center) and at the headquarters of the US Department of Defense (Pentagon) killed approximately 3000 (with many more injured). In the aftermath, the US initiated its 'War on Terror' and this was an opportunity for former opponents of the US (such as China and Russia) to join the counter-terrorism alliance. China seized this opportunity to join US anti-terrorist programmes while at the same time using this shift in threat perceptions to non-traditional threats to build new security partnerships in Central Asia.

The administration of China's current paramount leader Xi Jinping, General Secretary of the Communist Party of China since 2012 and President of the People's Republic of China since 2013, has to been seen against this historical background. Xi is the leader who introduced the vision of a New Silk Road (the Belt and Road Initiative) but the groundwork has already been laid by the preceding administrations. The BRI is a fascinating geopolitical project of our time—the setting, the prequel for this project to come to life, is even more interesting.

Russia

The Soviet Union suffered in the 1990s what many pro-Soviet analysts assess as the worst humiliation in the long Russian history. Having been the superpower counterpart of the US for decades, Soviet Union's break-up was not only a disaster in terms of power and territory (several Soviet republics declared independence) but also a watershed in terms of security and economic alliances. Of the three major powers (i.e., the US, China, and Russia), Russia surely lost the most of power and influence in this period, and thus offered the US and China spaces to occupy in terms of political and security partnerships and economic cooperation.

The Soviet invasion of Afghanistan (1979–1989) was probably Part I of the decline, the beginning of the end. The USSR felt overstretched in terms of military personnel and military material deployed there, partly due to the hostile, mountainous terrain, partly due to the long periods of fighting, and partly due to the covert US support for the Afghan fighters. In sum, the superpower USSR came close to a humiliating defeat and left Afghanistan without reaching its goal of gaining control there.

The end of the Cold War followed suit. Beginning with the election of a non-communist opposition government in Poland in June 1989, several other revolutionary acts ended Soviet power in Eastern European countries, with the climax being the fall of the Berlin Wall in November 1989. The non-violent revolutions were only possible because they were tolerated by the Soviet leader Mikhail Gorbachev (1985–1991), who was willing to change the USSR with the programmes of 'Glasnost' (openness and transparency) and 'Perestroika' (restructuring) and who did not militarily suppress the mass demonstrations in Eastern Europe. But the turmoil of change and the nationalist resentments against his programmes led to an attempted coup, which failed but resulted in the resignation of Gorbachev.

He was followed by Boris Yeltsin (Russian President from 1991 to 1999), but during his administration, chaotic struggles for (economic) power and profits never could be hedged and the 1990s became a decade of internal instability and economic decline for Russia. Succeeding the devastating Soviet invasion in Afghanistan came the First Chechen War (December 1994–August 1996). Despite Russian superiority in regard to manpower and military material deployed, the Chechen guerrilla warfare demoralised the Russian forces and in combination with negative public opinion in Russia on this military mission President Yeltsin signed a ceasefire in 1996.

But the conflict was not resolved, and by August 1999, Russia entered the Second Chechen War (which lasted until April 2009). Officially, they were counter-terrorist operations on territories of the North Caucasian region (in line with the global anti-terror programmes initiated mainly by the US' War on Terror).

Overall, the Yeltsin administration was a period in Russian history of decline in economic terms and in regard to its status as a superpower. The Chechen wars occupied political and military resources that limited Russia's options in other regions.

In regard to security alliances, Russia initiated the Collective Security Treaty Organization (CSTO), founded in 1992. Besides Russia, the other CSTO founding members were Armenia, Kazakhstan, Kyrgyzstan, Tajikistan, and Uzbekistan. The CSTO was mainly founded as a hedge against the North Atlantic Treaty Organization's (NATO) further expansion, since members of the CSTO would not be able to join other military alliances.

The successor of President Yeltsin was the director of Russia's secret service (FSB, formerly known as KGB) Vladimir Putin. When Yeltsin resigned in 1999, Putin stepped in. He was President of Russia from 2000 to 2008 and, after a constitutionally required break, has again been since 2012. Similar to his Chinese counterpart Xi, Putin benefitted from the changed political setting in international affairs after 9/11 and managed to improve relations with the West in general and the US in particular.

Improvement of Sino-Russian Relations

In the mid-1980s, Sino-Soviet relations started to improve, evidence for this rapprochement being the Chinese reduction of military forces along the Sino-Soviet borders between 1982 and 1986.

During the Gorbachev administration, relations further intensified and Sino-Soviet border talks were initiated in 1987. Troop reductions and confidence-building measures followed, and due to the impact of the US forces' domination in the First Gulf War in 1991, the perceived necessity to cooperate in respect of developing US hegemony contributed to the improvement of Sino-Russian relations (Chung 2004).

US

For the US, the dissolution of its decade-long arch-enemy Soviet Union was naturally a great opportunity to increase its sphere of influence. Following the logic of a zero-sum game, the obvious incapability of the former superpower USSR to support and protect its allies offered potentials for new partnerships in Western-led organisations.

After the end of the Cold War and Germany's reunification, the US sphere of influence in Eastern Europe successively increased. One method was via direct partnership in the US-led Western security alliance North Atlantic Treaty Organization (NATO). East Germany became a member in the course of German reunification in 1990. In the aftermath of this event, the NATO had been aggrandised in three waves eastwards with the accession of Poland, Hungary, and the Czech Republic in 1999. All three countries had formerly been member states of the rival 'Warsaw Pact' from 1955 to 1991.

In 2004, the next round of NATO enlargement included Estonia, Latvia, and Lithuania as well as Slovakia, Slovenia, Romania, and Bulgaria. All, with the exception of Slovenia, had also been members of the USSR-led Warsaw Pact from 1955 to 1991.

Finally, in 2009, Albania and Croatia became NATO members, of which Albania had formerly been a Warsaw Pact member. The US has thus been able to seize the geostrategic opportunity in Europe, which the dissolution of the former USSR and the weakness of its follow-on state Russia offered in the aftermath of the Cold War.

Another vehicle was through the NATO programme for eastward enlargement called 'Partnership for Peace' (PfP), which focused directly on Eastern European and Central Asian states that formerly belonged to the Warsaw Pact. PfP is a NATO programme, designed to establish trustful relationships via military-to-military cooperation, and unofficially an avenue towards full NATO membership. The aforementioned new East European NATO members had been members of the PfP programme prior to their NATO membership.

Established in 1994, the PfP comprises twelve former republics of the Soviet Union—one of them Russia itself. Kazakhstan, Kyrgyzstan, Tajikistan, and Russia became PfP members in 1994—only two years before the foundation of the Shanghai Five, the predecessor of the Shanghai Cooperation Organisation. This is an example of how smaller Central Asian states tried to evaluate and seize their best options in the major power game between the US, China, and Russia.

After the collapse of the Soviet Union, the US remained the sole superpower since China was still in the development stage in the 1990s as was the European Union back then.

- The administration of George Bush Senior (1989–1993) was defined by the unique event of the USSR's dissolution and the new opportunities for the US to gain influence in Eastern Europe.
- President Bill Clinton (1993–2001) tried to further expand the US spheres of influence into the Central Asian regions.
- The administration of George Bush Junior (2001–2009) was massively impacted by the terrorist attacks of 9/11, and in the following years, the focus of US foreign policy shifted towards non-traditional threats (as opposed to the former state actor threat perceptions) (Barnett 2005).

Central Asia: Political

For Central Asian states, the 1990s was a decade of immense transformation; many gained independence from the former Soviet Union at the beginning of the 1990s and had to build up proper political, economic, and security systems, including a foreign affairs policy. Naturally, the strings to Russia on all levels remained strong.

Kazakhstan

Geography

Kazakhstan is located in Central Asia with, geographically, its eastern part being located on the European continent. Its geographic location makes it the perfect transit country for China westwards to Western Europe. Kazakhstan shares an almost 1800 kilometres long border with China, more precisely with China's Xinjiang region. Furthermore, Kazakhstan has borders with Russia, Kyrgyzstan, Uzbekistan, and Turkmenistan and thus is the geographic centre of Central Asia and the SCO.

Politics

Kazakhstan declared independence from the USSR on 16 December 1991, and since then, Nursultan Nazarbayev had been President of Kazakhstan for the next three decades. During the phase of gaining independence from the USSR, it was Nazarbayev who invited the leaders of the four Central Asian states Kyrgyzstan, Tajikistan, Turkmenistan, and Uzbekistan to discuss the possibility of building a Turkic confederation. This plan failed, but demonstrates the political closeness of these states, which later will build the Central Asian bloc of the Shanghai Five and the SCO.

Kazakhstan however maintained strong relations with Russia; it was the last of the Central Asian states to declare independence from the USSR. Besides nuclear warheads, Kazakhstan is home of the Baikonur Cosmodrome, the world's first and largest space launch facility, built by the USSR and now leased to Russia (until 2050). It has traditionally sold petroleum and natural gas to Russia at artificially low prices and allowed Russian companies (e.g., Lukoil and Gazprom) to invest freely in Kazakhstan.

Economy

Despite the political insecurity and collapse of trade relations formerly centered on the Soviet Union, Kazakhstan managed to overcome the especially economically turbulent first years of independence. The main source of income for Kazakhstan is the exports of natural resources. The exports of Kazakhstan declined in the early 1990s to a low level, at below US$4 billion per year.

In 1995, it exported goods worth US$1.2 billion. Of these exports, refined petroleum accounted for only 5.6 per cent and crude petroleum for 3.7 per cent. The export of petroleum gas was not existent.

Nowadays (2017) Kazakhstan exports goods amounting to US$44 billion, which is a decisive decrease compared to the record year 2012 when the value of exports amounted to US$83.8 billion. The export of natural resources remains the driver of Kazakhstan's economy. Over 50 per cent of Kazakhstan's exports are oil and gas, with 45 per cent being crude petroleum, 5.4 per cent petroleum gas, and 2.7 per cent refined petroleum. The main destinations for Kazakhstan's exports are China (13 per cent) and Russia (11 per cent), followed by France (7.6 per cent), the Netherlands (7.3 per cent), and Germany (4.3 per cent).[1]

Military/Security: Strategic Alliances

Strategically, Kazakhstan first tried to benefit from an ambivalent style of foreign relations in regard to the two superpowers (i.e., the US and Russia as USSR's successor) and later towards China as well. It developed a close defence relationship with the US and was a member in the NATO's Partnership for Peace (PfP) programme. Kazakhstan joined the US in its War on Terror and received in return training and security assistance from the US, which played a crucial role in developing its anti-terror capabilities. Kazakhstan was also a founding member of the CSTO (initiated by Russia) and of the Shanghai Five (initiated by China).

[1] https://oec.world/en/profile/country/kaz/#Exports

Uzbekistan

Geography

As a double landlocked country (i.e., Uzbekistan is surrounded by countries that are landlocked themselves), it was especially difficult for Uzbekistan to develop trade routes of its own without access to international sea lines. Uzbekistan is inhabited by 32 million people and the neighbouring countries are Kazakhstan, Afghanistan, Turkmenistan, Tajikistan, and Kyrgyzstan.

Politics

Uzbekistan declared independence from the USSR on 31 August 1991, and shortly after, Islam Karimov became the first President of Uzbekistan—a position he held on to until his death in 2016. Uzbekistan, as all the former Soviet satellites, was economically highly dependent on the USSR. After the collapse of the USSR, Uzbekistan had troubles in developing a proper economy and trade relations alternative to the USSR.

Economy

In 1992, the total of Uzbekistan's exports amounted to merely US$194 million, of which 86 per cent was raw cotton exports. By 1996, the Uzbek exports had substantially increased to a total amount of US$2.3 billion. Russia was still the number one export destination for Uzbekistan (25 per cent of Uzbek exports), followed by Italy (9.9 per cent), South Korea (7.6 per cent), and the US (6.4 per cent). Raw cotton remained the most important export commodity, with a share of 59 per cent of Uzbek exports in 1996, but this share decreased and was partly replaced by mining products (gold and copper; Uzbekistan possesses the fourth-largest gold deposits in the world) and agricultural products.[2]

[2] https://oec.world/en/visualize/tree_map/sitc/export/uzb/all/show/1996/

Military/Security: Strategic Alliances

Uzbekistan developed a special security relationship with the US beginning in the 1990s. The partnership included training of military personnel—Uzbekistan's army is the biggest of the Central Asian states.

Following 9/11, Uzbekistan joined the US in its global War on Terror and allowed the US to operate an airfield in Karshi-Khanabad. This partnership soon came to an end when the US condemned the Uzbek handling of civil unrest in Andijan (labelled afterwards the 'Andijan massacre'), and in 2005 the US troops left Uzbekistan.

Kyrgyzstan

Geography

Kyrgyzstan is a landlocked country, neighbouring China, Kazakhstan, Uzbekistan, and Tajikistan. The mountainous country is home to 6.4 million inhabitants. Only eight per cent of the land is cultivated but Kyrgyzstan possesses significant amounts of rare earth metals and gold. Besides Kazakhstan, Kyrgyzstan is the only country in Central Asia where Russian is an official language.

Politics

Kyrgyzstan declared independence from the USSR on 31 August 1991, and from then until 2005, President Askar Akayev ruled the country before the so-called 'Tulip Revolution' ended his administration. He was followed by President Kurmanbek Bakiyev, but Bakiyev was unsuccessful in pacifying the troubled Kyrgyz society and had to flee the country in 2010.

Economy

Kyrgyzstan's economy was in a difficult situation after the collapse of the USSR, similar to all other former Soviet satellites. In 1994, the total amount of Kyrgyz exports amounted to merely US$112 million. The Kyrgyz export commodities comprised non-iron waste (12 per cent), unwrought base metals (10 per cent), greasy wool (9.3 per cent), raw cotton (8 per cent), raw calf skin (6 per cent), and raw sheep skin (5.3 per cent). The economic productivity was back to a very low level. The overwhelming part of Kyrgyzstan's exports in 1994 went to China (61 per cent) followed, with a large distance, by exports to France (7 per cent), the US (6.3 per cent), and Germany (5.8 per cent).

In 2016, the agricultural production and especially the mining industry contributed to increase Kyrgyz exports to a total of US$1.38 billion, with gold (51 per cent) accounting for the majority of the export income. The main destination of Kyrgyz exports is now Switzerland (47 per cent).[3]

Military/Security: Strategic Alliances

Kyrgyzstan relies heavily on its Russian partnership in regard to security policies. In 2002, the countries signed a new security pact, following which Russia deployed fighter aircraft (Su-25 and Su-27 fighter jets) to its airbase in Kyrgyzstan. It is one of the largest troop deployments outside of Russia and an expression of the close security relations between the two countries.

Tajikistan

Geography

Tajikistan is, like the other Central Asian countries, a landlocked country without direct access to international waters. It neighbours China, Afghanistan, Uzbekistan, and Kyrgyzstan and is home for approximately 9.2 million people.

Politics

Tajikistan declared independence from the USSR on 9 September 1991 and was in the aftermath troubled by a civil war (1992–1997). Since 1994, Emomali Rahmon has been President of Tajikistan.

Economics

In 1997, the year a ceasefire for the civil war was agreed upon, the Tajik exports amounted to US$268 million. The main commodities of

[3] https://oec.world/en/visualize/tree_map/sitc/export/kgz/show/all/2016/

Tajikistan's exports then were raw cotton (44 per cent), raw aluminium (8.6 per cent), and dried fruits (7.1 per cent). Russia was Tajikistan's main destination for exports (35 per cent), followed by Italy (11 per cent), France (7.8 per cent), and Spain (5 per cent).

By 2017, Tajikistan's exports had become much more diversified, as a result of the economic development, and the total exports amounted to a value of US$940 million. Raw aluminium (18 per cent), gold (17 per cent), zinc ore (15 per cent), and lead ore (12 per cent) are now the most important commodities of Tajikistan's exports. The most important export destinations for Tajikistan in 2017 were Kazakhstan (32 per cent), Turkey (21 per cent), and Switzerland (17 per cent).[4]

Military/Security: Strategic Alliances

The security situation in Tajikistan is somewhat similar to that in Kyrgyzstan, with Russia as the security guarantor. The number of Russian troops stationed in Tajikistan is even greater than the Russian troops in Kyrgyzstan, due to the fact that Tajikistan shares a border with Afghanistan in the Pamir Mountains. The unsecure border with Afghanistan has led to the high number of Russian border guards deployed there, making Tajikistan the country with the highest number of Russian troops stationed outside of Russia.

Economics: The Setting

China suffered from international isolation following the Tian'anmen Square protests. The US cancelled its economic aid programme worth US$5 billion as did the EU. The World Bank suspended loans and the EU started (together with the US) an arms embargo.

This situation substantially improved in the new millennium, especially after 2001 and the War on Terror. China could steadily increase its integration in the global economic system and benefitted from the opportunities to enter new markets with its semi-manufactured goods.

Russia's economy suffered in the 1990s from the collapse of the Soviet Union's established trade system but recovered, similar to China, in the new millennium. The export of natural resources especially guaranteed the rise of Russia's economy as a whole.

[4] https://oec.world/en/visualize/tree_map/hs92/export/tjk/show/all/2017/

The Central Asian states, especially the former Soviet republics, suffered in the 1990s from the economic weakness of the USSR's successor Russia, since the USSR was their single most important trade partner. The resurgence of both the Russian and Chinese economy offered new opportunities for the Central Asian states, especially for Kazakhstan, Uzbekistan, Kyrgyzstan, and Tajikistan.

Security: The Setting

Threat Perceptions in Central Asia

Central Asia has gained an increasingly important position in the system of geopolitical analyses because of its strategic location between Asia and Europe, its reserves of fossil fuels, and its multiethnic societies. The nature of conflict in Central Asia has been defined as the new 'Great Game' by Peter Hopkirk, the 'Grand Chessboard' by Zbigniew Brzezinski, and the origin of Samuel Huntington's 'Clash of Civilizations'.

As a legacy of various colonial and Soviet occupations, the border demarcations often ignore the territorial location of ethnic groups; indeed, demarcations were even deliberately chosen to divide ethnic groups. Central Asia has been the theatre of major powers' interests for over two centuries, and mutual suspicions among the Central Asian states and especially in regard to major powers' interference originate from this 'Great Game'.

In the following, the various threat perceptions of the SCO members are outlined to identify common interests, opportunities for cooperation, and possible obstacles for a deepened multilateral cooperation.

'China Threat'

China has been seen as a threat in the region especially due to its complicated relationship with the Soviet Union during the Mao era. The perception of China improved in the context of the Sino-Soviet rapprochement beginning in the 1980s—the resolution of the Sino-Soviet border dispute and the demilitarisation of the border regions being a milestone.

Following the Sino-Soviet border war of 1969, the situation became very unstable and resulted in various (minor) border incidents. The border was heavily armed, and mutual threat perceptions by Soviet and Chinese leaders characterised the relationship during the 1970s. It was only in the

1980s that a shift in perception (caused by a shift in Chinese and Soviet leadership) improved the Sino-Soviet relations, which resulted in a rapprochement. Due to the improved political relations, in 1982 cross-border cooperation and limited border trade between China and the Soviet Union was resumed. An expression of the political détente was the mutual withdrawal of 80,000 troops from the Soviet and Chinese borders.

It has to be noted, however, that the character of a perceived 'China threat' was not limited to the military realm (this part improved substantially) but concerned economic and demographic aspects as well. China's economy is significantly superior to that of its Central Asian neighbours, as well as of Russia, and Chinese state-owned enterprises are capable of outperforming their Central Asian counterparts. The fear that China will use its economic prowess to dictate economic conditions on its terms contributed to a perceived China threat. Economic concerns reached their climax in the aftermath of the Soviet Union's dissolution and the subsequent fall of the Russian GDP in 1991. In addition, after the opening of the Sino-Soviet border in 1988 to foster economic cooperation, Chinese workers entered the Russian Far East region in large numbers in search of income opportunities. The immigration of Chinese workers raised fears of a consequent Chinese domination of the region since in the mid-1990s the Russian population east of Lake Baikal was under 7 million but China's population in the border region accumulated to 94 million.

China identified the necessity to address these multilevel concerns in order to establish a stable environment for economic development along its borders. A multilateral discussion forum such as the Shanghai Five was an appropriate means to downplay concerns regarding a rising China threat.

Russia as a Threat

Russia's dominating role in Central Asia originates from its former position during the Soviet Union. The Central Asian states rely economically to a huge degree on trade relations with Russia and base their security systems on Russian support and supply. Russia itself has steadily increased its defence budget and maintained an unchallenged military superiority compared to its Central Asian neighbours. Additionally, in the Central Asian states of Kazakhstan, Kyrgyzstan, and Tajikistan numerous groups of Russian immigrants exist, who constitute a noticeable part of the domestic public opinion. In Kazakhstan, this group represents 38 per cent of the population, while in Kyrgyzstan Russian migrants amount to 22 per cent. Tajikistan's number of Russian migrants has been reduced due to the impacts of the civil war.

Russia's treatment of the Central Asian region as a sphere of special interest (sometimes labelled as 'Russia's backyard') and its efforts to exclude external (i.e., US) influence in the region have increased concerns among Central Asian policymakers in regard to maintaining sovereign policy options. As part of a diversifying strategy, the Central Asian countries have reached out to China as an alliance option to Russia and are even trying to develop relationships with external actors to balance a Sino-Russian domination of the region.

Separatism-Terrorism Problematic in Central Asia

For China, the problem of separatist movements and (Islamic) terrorism in the Central Asian region is related to activities of the Uyghur minority in Xinjiang (新疆 – Xīnjiāng) and the neighbouring countries. The sparsely populated Xinjiang autonomous region is inhabited mainly by the Uyghur people, a Muslim minority in China. Despite efforts of the Chinese government to increase the percentage of Han Chinese in the region, the Uyghur maintained a separatist campaign and attracted support from Muslim groups in the region (e.g., from the East Turkestan Islamic Movement, or ETIM), much to the displeasure of Beijing's policymakers. For example, about 400,000 Uyghurs are estimated to be living in Kazakhstan and Kyrgyzstan, which are out of reach for China.

The history of Uyghur uprising can be traced back as long as to the nineteenth century; Chung Chien-peng dates the first major event in the year of 1865. Terrorist activities of the Uyghur separatist movement gained momentum in the mid-1990s, including bomb attacks in Urumqi and Beijing. Fifteen bomb attacks have been counted in 1998 and another seven in 1999. China therefore pushed for bilateral and multilateral cooperation with its Central Asian neighbours to address separatist Uyghur activities.

For Russia, the most troubling security threats in the region stem from ethnic uprisings in its southern regions, namely Chechnya. Following the dissolution of the Soviet Union, separatist movements in Chechnya gained momentum and unleashed a harsh reaction from Russian policymakers, resulting in the Russo-Chechen war of 1994–1996. Tensions never ceased and caused a subsequent full-scale war in 1999, including the bombardment of Chechen cities and refugee flows within the region.

The Central Asian states have experienced occasional outbreaks of inter-clan, inter-ethnic, and inter-religious conflicts. Sometimes the governments even blamed each other for supporting armed terrorist groups on the opponents' territory. During the civil war in Tajikistan from 1992 to 1997, the Tajik government accused the Uzbeks of supporting insurgents (i.e., the United Tajik Opposition) who operated from the Uzbek soil. Uzbekistan itself deployed armed troops on Tajik territory to fight Islamist insurgents who entered Uzbekistan from Afghanistan via Tajikistan. In Kyrgyzstan, the Uzbek minority has become a source of instability in Kyrgyzstan's south.

In general, it can be stated that the security threats in the Central Asian region are rather non-traditional in nature instead of interstate and are often caused by transborder communities, thus requiring a multilateral approach.

The experiences of the so-called 'Rose Revolution' in Georgia in 2003, the 'Orange Revolution' in Ukraine in 2004, and the 'Tulip Revolution' in Kyrgyzstan in 2005 heightened the fears of autocratic governments and intensified the combined efforts to suppress such movements.

In this regard, the various groups of insurgents increased the policymakers' willingness to foster inter-governmental security cooperation. Accordingly, Uzbekistan's application for SCO membership was directly motivated by terrorist threats posed by the Islamic Movement of Uzbekistan (IMU), Uyghur groups, and the Taleban.

Afghanistan-Related Threats

The ongoing insurgencies in Afghanistan pose a permanent threat to the Central Asian states due to the states' insufficient capabilities to secure their borders from illegal invasion. Afghanistan's direct neighbours Uzbekistan and Turkmenistan (which is not even affiliated with the SCO as an observer state) especially fear the involvement of Islamic terrorist groups in its countries. The Islamic Movement of Uzbekistan (IMU) and the East Turkestan Islamic Movement (ETIM) are two terrorist groups noteworthy in this regard which are active in Afghanistan but originate in the neighbouring countries.

Substantial economic income is gained through criminal activities in the region, for example, by the lucrative drug trafficking originating in Afghanistan. The Central Asian states are located between the world's largest supplier of heroin (i.e., Afghanistan) and the regions of its highest consumption, which are Russia and Europe. A United Nations Office on Drugs and Crime report assessed that 85 per cent of opiates transiting Central Asia passed through Tajikistan. The transit routes northwards hamper the security of the neighbouring states, especially since regional elites and corrupt officials participate in and benefit from these activities. In this regard, Tajikistan and Uzbekistan are the countries most troubled by drug trafficking. According to a World Bank report, one-third of the countries' GDP is related to drug trafficking.

Besides the destabilising impact on border control efforts and development of the economies in the region, the illegal drug trafficking provides a lucrative refunding possibility for regional terrorist groups. Hence, the non-traditional threats originating in Afghanistan (terrorism and drug trafficking) fostered the inter-governmental security cooperation of the Central Asian states with China and Russia.

'Three Evils' (三股势力)

The term 'three evils', coined by the PRC leadership, refers to the perceived threats in the region, namely terrorism, extremism, and separatism. When the Chinese term is translated, it means 'three forces/powers/influences' but was eventually translated as 'three evils'. As various critics have noted, the definition of these threats is rather imprecise and thus allows the governments of the SCO members to suppress dissidents and insurgents in the same manner.

In the mid-1990s, and related to the crisis in Taleban-controlled Afghanistan that spilled security threats all over the region, the so-called three evils increased in the importance of threat perceptions of regional policymakers. At its third summit, the Shanghai Five members issued a joint communiqué to address the threat of the three (evil) forces and the criminal activities of drug and arms smuggling.

As a result of the strategic shift towards non-traditional threats, the Shanghai Five Forum, which was focused on border security concerns, was transformed into the Shanghai Cooperation Organisation to address these threats in a concerted effort.

In the 'Shanghai Convention on Combating Terrorism, Separatism and Extremism', agreed on in 2001, the 'three evils' are defined as follows:

> (…) 1. >terrorism< means: any act recognized as an offence in one of the treaties listed in the Annex to this Convention […] and as defined in this

> Treaty; other act intended to cause death or serious bodily injury to a civilian, or any other person not taking an active part in the hostilities in a situation of armed conflict or to cause major damage to any material facility, as well as to organize, plan, aid and abet such act, when the purpose of such act, by its nature or context, is to intimidate a population, violate public security or to compel public authorities or an international organization to do or to abstain from doing any act, and prosecuted in accordance with the national laws of the Parties;
>
> 2. >separatism< means any act intended to violate territorial integrity of a State including by annexation of any part of its territory or to disintegrate a State, committed in a violent manner, as well as planning and preparing, and abetting such act, and subject to criminal prosecuting in accordance with the national laws of the Parties;
>
> 3. >extremism< is an act aimed at seizing or keeping power through the use of violence or changing violently the constitutional regime of a State, as well as a violent encroachment upon public security, including organization, for the above purposes, of illegal armed formations and participation in them, criminally prosecuted in conformity with the national laws of the Parties.[5]

The Shanghai Convention on Combating Terrorism, Separatism and Extremism was signed the day the SCO was formed, on 15 June 2001, an indicator of the importance the SCO members assigned to the problem of the three evils. This focus on non-traditional security threats eventually led to the establishment of the Regional Anti-Terrorist Structure (RATS), headquartered in Tashkent, Uzbekistan.[6]

China's approach to address the three evils includes, besides security-related efforts, a programme called 'Open Door Policy' (改革开放—Gǎigé kāifàng), which focuses on improving economic relations and trade with China's neighbours. The Open Door Policy is especially designed to improve the economic conditions in Xinjiang and has succeeded in attracting investment and entrepreneurs from its neighbouring countries as well as within China from its western provinces.

[5] 'Shanghai Convention on Combating Terrorism, Separatism and Extremism', available at: www.eurasiangroup.org/files/documents/conventions_eng/The_20Shanghai_20Convention

[6] For more details about RATS and the institutionalisation process of the SCO see Chap. 7 of this book.

The collapse of the USSR was the end for the established security architecture in Central Asia; the waning of the superpower security guarantor sent whole regions into de facto anarchy. Additionally, the newly independent states of Central Asia had border issues to resolve and the entire border security had to be established.

The overall chaotic setting in Central Asia that followed the collapse of the Soviet Union opened windows of opportunities in the realms of political, economic, and security cooperation. How central the foundation of the Shanghai Five and its successor, the Shanghai Cooperation Organisation, was for China to prepare the ground for its Belt and Road Initiative is assessed in the following chapter.

Bibliography

Aron, Leon. 2013. The Putin Doctrine – Russia's Quest to Rebuild the Soviet State. Foreign Affairs

Barnett, Thomas P.M. 2005. The Pentagon's New Map – War and Peace in the Twenty-First Century. New York: Penguin Group

Brzezinski, Brzezinski. 1998. The Grand Chessboard – American Primacy and its Geostrategic Imperatives. New York: Basic Books

Chung, Chien-Peng. 2004. Domestic Politics, International Bargaining and China's Territorial Disputes. London + New York: RoutledgeCurzon

Hopkirk, Peter. 1994. The Great Game – The Struggle for Empire in Central Asia. Tokyo: Kodansha International

Huntington, Samuel. 1996. The Clash of Civilizations and the Remaking of World Order. New York: Simon & Schuster

Kleveman, Lutz. 2004. New Great Game – Blood and Oil in Central Asia. New York + London: Grove Press

Lateigne, Marc. 2005. China in international institutions – alternate paths to global power. Abingdon + New York: Routledge

Pradt, Tilman. 2016. China's New Foreign Policy. London: Palgrave Macmillan

CHAPTER 3

Introduction to Shanghai Five (and SCO)

On 26 April 1996, the heads of state of the five countries China, Russia, Kazakhstan, Kyrgyzstan, and Tajikistan met in Shanghai to discuss security confidence-building measures along their shared borders and to resolve existing border disputes. This was the founding meeting of the multilateral club named Shanghai Five, the predecessor of the Shanghai Cooperation Organisation (SCO).

China shares a border of over 7000 kilometres with these neighbours and the history of these borders was often conflicted. China and Russia were especially engaged in border fighting, for example, in 1969 about the disputed Damansky Island (Zhenbao in Chinese) located in the Ussuri River on the border between Russia and China. During the Cold War, the Russian-Chinese border was in general suspiciously observed and both countries stationed heavily armed troops on their side due to the conflicted character of their relations.

Improvement of Sino-Russian Relations

In the mid-1980s, Sino-Soviet relations started to improve, evidence for this rapprochement being the Chinese reduction of military forces along the Sino-Soviet borders between 1982 and 1986.

During the Gorbachev administration, relations further intensified and Sino-Soviet border talks were initiated in 1987. Troop reductions and confidence-building measures followed, and due to the impact of the US

T. Pradt, *The Prequel to China's New Silk Road*,
https://doi.org/10.1007/978-981-15-4708-9_3

forces' domination in the First Gulf War in 1991, the perceived necessity to cooperate in regard to developing US hegemony contributed to the improvement of Sino-Russian relations.

The new level of confidence was manifested by the delivery of modern weapon systems from Russia for China's People's Liberation Army beginning in the early 1990s.

This first meeting and all subsequent Shanghai Five meetings were meant to foster trust among the neighbours and set the preconditions for bilateral talks to resolve their border disputes.

As first steps to increase transparency and as confidence-building measures, the members of the Shanghai Five agreed to limit the scale and frequency of military exercises in the vicinity of the borders, to invite foreign military officers to observe military exercises, and to employ similar measures to increase the exchange between the various militaries and thus decrease the existing friction.

During their second Shanghai Five meeting, on 24 April 1997, the member states agreed to reduce their military forces stationed along their borders. Furthermore, the character of military equipment in the border areas changed to solely defensive material. These changes, reached within a short period of only one year, led to a substantial change for the better with respect to the border disputes, improved the relations among the members, and fostered the overall development of the Shanghai Five.

The member states shared their interest in deepening economic cooperation, and to foster their trade relations, further, they considered the threats of national separatism, international terrorism, and religious extremism to be the crucial security challenges of the region that needed to be addressed. These shared values and the mutual respect for the territorial sovereignty of the member states have been the foundation on which the success of the Shanghai Five was built. Also, the institutionalisation process was fostered, on their fifth meeting in 2000, when the establishment of a council to coordinate the various annual meetings (e.g., annual meeting of the member states' foreign and defence ministers) was agreed upon.

The progress reached within the framework of the Shanghai Five in only five years was impressive and led to a lasting improvement of the economic cooperation, (eventually) to the solution of border conflicts, and in general to increased security in the border regions. Which drivers fostered this process and helped to overcome the protracted border conflicts? Since questions about demarcations and delimitations of borders are directly interwoven with questions of national sovereignty, and often national identity, the solving of border conflicts is complicated—all the more so in situations when the opponents are perceived threats and any claimant has to avoid the appearance of weakness. In an environment of insecurity about the opponent's ambitions, the chances for border regulations with one side offering concessions are low.

In the given situation of the mid-1990s, the main players of this region, namely China and Russia, were troubled with other geopolitical challenges. Russia had to struggle with the consequences of the collapse of the USSR and China was internationally isolated due to the 'Taiwan Strait Crisis' of 1995–1996 and hence suffered economic sanctions. Both countries had therefore a strong motivation to improve the situation along their borders, to decrease the threat level, and thus be able to dramatically reduce the military troops and equipment stationed there. Moreover, Russia and China understood that their border regions would not be stable and secure as long as their neighbouring Central Asian countries were weak and unstable. Additionally, the US was seeking to expand its sphere of influence eastwards (via the NATO Partnership for Peace programme among others)—a development both Russia and China could not accept. The objective to address non-traditional security threats (read terrorism), to build a counterweight to US influence, and to foster economic cooperation among them unified the members of the Shanghai Five and led to further institutionalisation of their relations, which resulted in the foundation of the SCO.

The SCO

The SCO encompasses most of the Central Asian region, taking the states with observer status into consideration; it spans from the Middle East to the South China Sea and to the north of Russia's Arctic borders. The six SCO founding member states (China, Russia, Kazakhstan, Kyrgyzstan, Tajikistan, and Uzbekistan) already encompassed a territory of around 30 million square kilometres (or three-fifths of the Eurasian continent) and represented a quarter of the world's population.

According to the US Department of Energy, the SCO founding member states and observer states combined possessed 17.5 per cent of the world's proven oil reserves and approximately 50 per cent of proven natural gas reserves. The combined oil production of the SCO founding members amounted to 20.3 per cent of global oil production, and their gas production constituted 24.3 per cent of the global gas production in 2010.

This map illustrates the geographical dimension of the SCO founding members and its then-observer states:[1]

China and Russia were by far the biggest founding members of the SCO, in terms of their size, population, economies, military, and political power. The Central Asian founding members Kazakhstan, Kyrgyzstan,

[1] Source: Bailes et al. (2007, #970).

Tajikistan, and, since 2001, Uzbekistan, can therefore only be classified as junior partners. They are nonetheless important for both China and Russia due to existing natural resources, the important geographic location (with important transportation lines), and especially being a source of security concerns. The newly independent Central Asian states faced a conflictual phase in economic and political terms after the demise of the Soviet Union.

Roughly half the population lived below the poverty line, unemployment rates remained high, weak security institutions were unable to contain organised crime, and neighbouring Afghanistan was a permanent source of further security threats.

After a period as observer states, in 2017, India and Pakistan became full members of the SCO. Together with these new members, the SCO now covers 60 per cent of the Eurasian continent and almost half of the global population. With Iran and Mongolia at the doorsteps (currently observer states) the SCO will only grow in geopolitical importance due to the further increased sphere of influence and as an 'Energy Club' when resource-rich Iran becomes a full member.

From China's perspective, the SCO provided the perfect frame to prepare the setting for its New Silk Road project called the 'Belt and Road Initiative' (BRI). The SCO member states encompass the landmass between China and Europe and are therefore the natural route for the land route (the 'Belt'). The mutual interest of the SCO member states to improve security, fight non-traditional security threats, and increase economic cooperation and trade via improved logistical connections—all these shared goals were in perfect accordance with the BRI to-do list.

China's Approach to SCO

First Steps in the 1990s

Sino-Russian relations steadily improved during the 1980s and were officially declared to be 'normal' by Soviet President Gorbachev during his visit to China in May 1989 (just shortly before the suppression of demonstrations on Tian'anmen Square on 4 June 1989).

The precursor of the Shanghai Cooperation Organisation (SCO), labelled the Shanghai Five, was established in 1996 and consisted of China, Russia, Kazakhstan, Kyrgyzstan, and Tajikistan. With the exception of Mongolia, this group represents all successor states of the former Soviet Union which share borders with China. In a transition phase from July

2000 to June 2001, the organisation was labelled the Shanghai Forum with the acceptance of Uzbekistan as the new member state. The organisation changed its name later to Shanghai Cooperation Organisation (SCO).

Economic Cooperation?

During the Sino-Soviet rapprochement and the following phase of establishing relations between the People's Republic of China (PRC) and the newly independent Central Asian states, the resolution of border disputes and questions of territorial sovereignty dominated the agenda of intergovernmental meetings. Once the border disputes were resolved, non-traditional security issues related to the developments in Afghanistan were the focus of the Shanghai Five and its successor, the SCO. Concepts of economic cooperation were foremost related to security issues (e.g., maintaining stability in Xinjiang) and did not pioneer the process of SCO institutionalisation.

Since economic cooperation was not the driving force during the foundation phase of the Shanghai Five and obviously not the main motivation for the establishment of this group, the following section analyses the motives of the various SCO members.

China's Motives

China's motives extended from improving the situation along the Sino-Russian border and further territorial conflicts to economic and energy interests in Central Asia. The Shanghai Five and later the SCO provided an opportunity to deepen relations with Russia and the other members in the political, economic, and security realms and thus possessed the capacity to contribute to an improved security environment. This would allow China to concentrate its efforts on continuing its economic growth and to focus on internal issues and offshore territorial disputes (i.e., Taiwan and the South China Sea).

To diversify its sources of energy supply, China was interested in developing oil and gas cooperation with the Central Asian states. Its trade with the Central Asian SCO members increased definitively since 1992 but remained negligible in the context of its energy demand. The importance of stable security and economic relations with Central Asia has to be understood in the context of China's Xinjiang situation. The amount of its trade with its Central Asian neighbours is only a fraction of its GDP but these trade relations are a crucial part of its strategy to maintain political and economic stability in its Xinjiang region. Therefore, China promoted the development of deepening economic relations within the Shanghai Five/SCO instead of solely focusing on security issues.

Furthermore, energy supply from the Central Asian sources, transported via a land transportation network, was not under the control of the US (in contrast to the sea lanes via the Indian Ocean) and thus would provide China with a strategic alternative in case of a future conflict with the US.

In regard to Russia's vigilance about China's activities in Central Asia, China identified multilateralism as the appropriate way to intensify relations with the newly independent Central Asian states without antagonising Russia.

China's participation in the Shanghai Five/SCO was also helpful in mitigating suspicions among its Central Asian neighbours about its future intentions and concerns about its growing political and military clout. Participation in this multilateral organisation was thus also meant to address discussions of a 'China threat' during the 1990s.

Russia's Motives and China's Rise

Russia had to realise a shift in the balance of power in relation to China's rise and its own relative decrease. Beginning in the 1980s and accelerated by both China's continued economic growth and the end of the Soviet Union, Russia was confronted with the reality that it no longer could treat China as its 'junior partner'.

In economic terms, the Russian economy required foreign investment, and to avoid a one-sided dependence on Western funds, China was the logical partner. But this Sino-Russian trade relation was designed to be bilateral and Russia was worried about China's increasing clout in Central Asia, both politically and in economic terms. For Russia, the Shanghai Five and subsequently the SCO was merely one regional organisation (besides the Commonwealth of Independent States (CIS), Collective Security Treaty Organization (CSTO), and Organization for Security and Co-operation in Europe (OSCE)) and Russia did not expect it to develop into the most important multilateral organisation in the region.

In security-related terms, the improvement of Sino-Russian relations and a relaxation of the situation along their shared borders allowed Russia to concentrate on other regional security concerns, primarily in the North Caucasus.

Russia has always been suspicious about growing Western influence in Central Asia (especially US engagement in the region) and, therefore, preferred an organisation which excluded non-regional actors.

The Central Asian States' Motives and China's Role

The paramount objective of the Central Asian member states of the SCO, especially in the 1990s, was to maintain their sovereignty and to avoid an overwhelming dependence on Russia. Joining a regional multilateral organisation together with China and Russia was therefore perceived as a viable opportunity to diversify political and economic relations.

This motive of diversification is also reflected in the Central Asian states' cooperation with the NATO via the Euro-Atlantic Partnership Council (EAPC) (formerly the North Atlantic Cooperation Council or NACC) and the NATO's Partnership for Peace (PfP) programme.

Kazakhstan, Kyrgyzstan, and Tajikistan joined the NACC in 1992. Kazakhstan and Kyrgyzstan joined the PfP in 1994, while Tajikistan followed in 2002. Uzbekistan, which became an SCO member in 2001, also joined the NACC and PfP in 1992 and 1994, respectively.[2] Besides participating in the NATO programmes, the Central Asian states of the SCO also cooperated with the OSCE and received substantial aid for developing their defence and intelligence-gathering capabilities.

Relying predominantly on the NATO and cooperating with Western countries meant the danger of alienating Russia. Therefore, the deepening of relations with China via the participation in a multilateral organisation provided the Central Asian states with an opportunity to diversify security relations without antagonising Russia. Furthermore, the participation in the SCO, in which both China and Russia were members, relieved the Central Asian states from a decision to choose between closer relations with only one of the two big regional powers.

In the economic realm, deepening trade relations with the growing Chinese economy and attracting Chinese FDI was very important for the Central Asian SCO members especially because of the Russian economy's downturn in the 1990s.

[2] See: https://www.nato.int/cps/en/natolive/51288.htm (accessed 2020/01/30).

Mutually Shared Motives

All SCO members share the (although varying) threat perception of Islamic independence movements. Declaring these groups as terrorists (especially in the aftermath of 9/11) helped to formulate a common policy and also contributed to the legitimisation of the SCO security cooperation efforts. Focusing on these threats allowed the members of the SCO as well as its predecessor the Shanghai Five to engage in confidence-building measures along its borders. The SCO attempted to address security concerns on two levels: the resolution of the border disputes improved the security in the region in terms of traditional threat definitions (state vs state), while the SCO agenda to fight the threats of terrorism, separatism, and extremism (the 'three evils') addressed non-traditional security threats (state vs non-state actors).

In economic terms, all SCO members are interested in strengthening trade relations in the region and participating in the emerging opportunities which China's economic rise provides, in terms of exports to China as well as attracting Chinese investments.

Institutionalisation

Similar to the Association of South East Asian Nations (ASEAN), the SCO members agree on the strict principle of non-interference in other members' internal affairs, a policy which is especially required by China but also appreciated by the authoritarian Central Asian SCO members. This basic understanding along with the Central Asian values (which are defined in distinction to Western values) has led to a working atmosphere which became coined as the 'Shanghai Spirit'.

The non-confrontational approach (consensus decision-making) in combination with the paramount non-interference dogma has resulted in a non-democratic atmosphere, and the overarching common interest of the SCO members' policymakers is to preserve their national power and sovereignty.

In respect of national sovereignty, however, the SCO institutionalisation process succeeded in establishing some supranational offices and bodies, which, for example, was never possible in regard to the China-ASEAN's institutionalisation process.

The important incentives were given at the annual summits and meetings of prime ministers and ministers. But below this senior Track-I level, a network of executive offices was established. In less than a decade, the SCO members had created a system of corresponding working groups mainly designed to foster intra-SCO trade and economic exchange, but aided by linkages to concerned political bodies (e.g., Council of Foreign Ministers). In this respect, the Meetings of Ministers and the Council of National Coordinators fulfil the roles of intersection points for associated working groups. These two bodies implement decisions taken at the senior level and coordinate these policies with the appropriate national bodies for execution.

Noteworthy in this regard is also the establishment of the SCO Secretariat (Beijing) and the Regional Anti-Terrorism Structure (RATS, Tashkent) in 2004. Both bodies possess their own staff (comprised of experts from all SCO member states) and own budget, although their independence remains symbolic. The Secretariat is the administrative body of the SCO, while RATS is the intelligence centre. Together, these two bodies are evidence for the materialised institutional process of the SCO, and besides being merely means of communication, they are an expression of the multilateral character of the SCO.

Another milestone of the SCO institutionalisation was the signing of the 'Convention on Counter-Terrorism' in 2009, a legal framework that aligned national regulations of the SCO members in order to facilitate cooperation in anti-terror efforts. By this Convention, the SCO members accepted restrictions on their sovereignties and domestic legislations for the sake of supranational anti-terror measures. This can arguably be considered a step towards building a security community.

Economic Cooperation

In the realm of economic cooperation, the SCO reached the maximum progress in the sector of energy cooperation (i.e., oil and gas). The development of infrastructure (e.g., railroads, highways, pipelines) was a necessary precondition for increasing regional trade and economic exchange. In this regard, China played a crucial role, initiating many infrastructure projects, supporting the SCO's Central Asian members with financial assistance packages, and becoming an important destination for natural resource exports. The Central Asian members benefitted from the economic cooperation efforts of the SCO; the development of the GDP and trade is interrelated with the SCO cooperation.

The trade balance between the Central Asian states and China, however, is disadvantageous for the Central Asian states, a fact which prevented the deepening of economic integration (i.e., an SCO Free Trade Agreement).

The high degree of economic interconnectedness, especially in the strategically sensible sector of energy security, has contributed to stabilising relations among the SCO members. But China's overwhelming economic domination might be the source of future conflicts if not properly adjusted.

Security Cooperation

The SCO reached considerable progress in the realm of security cooperation, in regard to both traditional confidence-building among its members and mutually perceived non-traditional threats (i.e., terrorism, separatism, and extremism).

However, some analysts criticise the lack of a concerted action, for example, the establishment of 'rapid intervention forces' to address upcoming crises in a member state or a collective security agenda for Afghanistan:

> If the SCO is viewed as a mechanism to reinforce confidence, it has been a historical success. But if it is viewed as an organization that attempts to influence Central Asian security realities, for the time being at least it appears to be no more than a "paper tiger". (Laruelle and Peyrouse 2013, p. 251)

By focusing on non-traditional security threats (i.e., the 'three evils'), the SCO managed to engage China and Russia with the smaller Central Asian states in security cooperation efforts without antagonising each other. The SCO contributed, therefore, not only to maintaining stable Sino-Russian relations but also to improved relations among its Central Asian members.

In the traditional security sector, the annual joint military exercises, 'Peace Mission', have further increased the security cooperation among the SCO members and have also functioned as a confidence-building measure. The formerly conflicted Sino-Russian relations have been improved (also) via joint military exercises, which are important sources of information about the other members' military development and therefore a means of transparency.

An expression of the growing mutual trust and evidence for the absence of a 'China threat' perception is the supply of sophisticated weapon systems especially from Russia to China. Weapon systems purchased by the Central Asian states is underdeveloped but this is due to the states' limited economic capabilities. The military-to-military relations in general have improved in regard to joint exercises, exchange of personnel, and information sharing. This has definitively contributed to reducing mutual suspicions, with again Sino-Russian relations predominantly being important in this respect.

Territorial Disputes

Contrary to the situation in the South China Sea, the territorial disputes among the Central Asian states were resolved before the deepening of relations. Some minor demarcation issues were postponed and only recently solved, but the majority of border disputes between the SCO members were successfully resolved in the 1990s.

The resolution of territorial disputes was therefore a precondition for deepened cooperation (ASEAN approach: deepened cooperation shall lead eventually to the resolution of territorial disputes).

Multilateralism

The SCO started as a forum for the discussion and negotiation of border disputes. The main task of its precursor, the Shanghai Five, was to improve communication with and interaction of the neighbouring countries in the region. The success of the Shanghai Five in terms of interaction and resolution of border disputes was the precondition for deepened multilateral relations. Thus, when the SCO was established in 2001, the basis for stable and prosperous relations was already set. Most of the territorial disputes were settled in the 1990s, further initiatives to increase security cooperation were launched, and in the economic realm, projects, especially in the energy sector, were agreed upon.

In the first decade of its existence, the SCO succeeded in institutionalising the multilateral relations of its members by the establishment of permanent bodies (e.g., secretariat and RATS), a system of corresponding working groups, and the initiation of steps towards a security community. Demonstrating the latter aspect are the various efforts of cooperation within the security realm and the related alignment of national laws to orchestrate the members' anti-terror efforts.

The progress of the SCO is, in fact, evidence of a working, bilateral Sino-Russian relationship with the Central Asian states as junior partners without much leverage. China and Russia possess the biggest political power, economies, and military capabilities and, therefore, naturally dominate the SCO. But given the members' different sizes, and economic and military clout, this phenomenon is not extraordinary for an organisation consisting of members that distinct. The progress of this organisation would not have been possible without a definite change (and improvement) of Sino-Russian relations in the 1990s.

In regard to the critical confidence-building steps (i.e., arms sales, border disputes, security cooperation) which were preconditions for deepening relations and the establishment of the SCO, the development of Sino-Russian relations was of paramount importance. In the process of the SCO's institutionalisation, it was China which forced many initiatives but again, without the support of Russia, these initiatives would not have been successful (as the example of a failed SCO Free Trade Agreement proves). Therefore, the SCO can be assessed as a regional organisation which is mainly dominated by Russia and China and thus, in its character, rather a bilateral than a multilateral organisation. The Central Asian states participate in (and benefit from) the SCO, but the agenda is set and decisions are taken by Russia and China. The SCO therefore bears testimony to China's preference of bilateral relationships instead of de facto multilateral groups.

The authors of a SIPRI study conclude in view of the crucial SCO characteristics:

> The smooth and complementary meshing of defensive elements in Russian motives with ambitions for 'soft'—that is, economic and cultural—hegemony on the Chinese side is the central secret of the SCO's success and the key to its hopes of survival. (Bailes 2007, p. 9)

* * *

Bibliography

Bailes, Alyson. J. K., & Dunay, Pál. 2007. The Shanghai Cooperation Organization as a regional security institution, SIPRI Policy Paper (Vol. 17, pp. 1–29). Stockholm: Stockholm International Peace Research Institute.

Garver, John W. 1989. The 'new type' of Sino-Soviet relations. Asian Survey, 29(12), 1136–1152.

Laanatza, Marianne. 2013. Central Asia, energy and Trade Politics from the SCO's Perspective. In M. Fredholm (Ed.) The Shanghai Cooperation Organization and Eurasian Geopolitics – New Directions, Perspectives, and Challenges (pp. 294–309). Copenhagen: NIAS Press.

Laruelle, Marlene & Peyrouse, Sebastien. 2013. Friendship with Moderation – The Central Asian Point of View on the SCO. In M. Fredholm (Ed.), The Shanghai Cooperation Organization and Eurasian Geopolitics – New Directions, Perspectives, and Challenges (pp. 229–252). Copenhagen: NIAS Press.

Swanström, Niklas. 2011. China and Greater Central Asia: New Frontiers?, Silk Road Paper. Stockholm + Washington, DC: Central Asia-Caucasus Institute.

Weitz, Richard. 2009. Growing Pains. The Journal of International Security Affairs (17).

Yu, Bin. 2013. The SCO Ten Years After – In Search of its Own Identity. In M. Fredholm (Ed.) The Shanghai Cooperation Organization and Eurasian Geopolitics – New Directions, Perspectives, and Challenges (pp. 29–61). Copenhagen: NIAS Press.

CHAPTER 4

Territorial Disputes in Central Asia

Territorial Disputes in Central Asia: A Brief Review

The border disputes between China and the former Soviet Union date back to the end of World War II. In 1969, at the disputed border area in Manchuria, a small island on the Ussuri River, the conflict between China and the Soviet Union escalated into military fighting, with several dozen soldiers killed or wounded.

Following the dissolution of the Soviet Union and the independence of its former satellite states, the border disputes became a multilateral issue. The border disputes in Central Asia were especially difficult to resolve since the administrative borders in Central Asia established by Moscow in the mid-1920s respected neither natural geographic nor ethnic boundaries. Therefore, the independence of the Central Asian states created a complex set of territorial claims while at the same time the newly established borders disrupted industrial and transportation links.

China shares a border of over 3300 kilometres with its Central Asian neighbours, mostly in mountainous terrain that is difficult to patrol. Therefore, the resolution of these border disputes was in accordance with China's policy to improve the security situation along its western borders to be able to focus on the security issues along its eastern shores and offshore.

For the later establishment of China's Silk Road Economic Belt project, the peaceful resolution of the protracted border conflicts in Central Asia was a crucial precondition. Without security in the border regions, no

T. Pradt, *The Prequel to China's New Silk Road*,
https://doi.org/10.1007/978-981-15-4708-9_4

establishment of infrastructure facilities, cross-border roads and railroads, would be possible. And without friendly relations between China and its Central Asian neighbours, the many unofficial bureaucratic means (e.g., lengthy controls, required documents) to prolong cross-border traffic would easily slow down any efforts to increase trade volumes in the region.

The historical dimensions of the various border conflicts in Central Asia and the unstable geopolitical situation in the 1990s did not facilitate any progress in these protracted disputes.

However, the mountainous terrain of the border regions also provided certain advantages for resolving the disputes. These areas were sparsely populated and demarcation shifts urged less public protests compared to other border regions.

In the aftermath of the dissolution of the Soviet Union and the independence of former Soviet regions, territorial disputes for the following sets of claimants emerged: Russia-China; Russia-Kazakhstan; Uzbekistan-Turkmenistan; Uzbekistan-Kazakhstan; Uzbekistan-Tajikistan; Uzbekistan-Kyrgyzstan; Kyrgyzstan-Tajikistan; Kyrgyzstan-China; Kyrgyzstan-Kazakhstan; Tajikistan-China; Tajikistan-Afghanistan; Kazakhstan-Turkmenistan; Turkmenistan-Afghanistan; and Kazakhstan-China.

In short, all of the later members of the Shanghai Cooperation Organisation (SCO) were involved in several cross-border disputes. The resolution of these border conflicts was on the one hand a required precondition for the establishment of the SCO. On the other hand, the peaceful and mutually respectful resolution process became the founding spirit of the SCO, a spirit of cooperation that stimulated deepening relations of the claimants and contributed to the success of the SCO on many levels, namely in the political, economic, and security realms.

The SCO (and even more, its predecessor, the Shanghai Five) offered a framework for the disputed parties to meet for confidence-building talks at first and explore the possibilities for deeper cooperation on various levels. In effect, the multilateral grouping was the means for the disputed claimants to cut through the 'Gordian knot' of their interwoven border disputes.

Resolved Border Disputes

During the 1990s, China reached agreements about its border disputes with the Soviet Union and, in the aftermath of its dissolution, with the successor states in Central Asia. The resolution of these border disputes allowed China to focus on other security issues, internal as well as external, especially after the incidents on Tian'anmen Square. Besides the 'security dividend' (China, as well as the other claimants to border conflicts, was able to substantially reduce the number of military troops positioned along its disputed borders), the resolution of border conflicts laid the groundwork for increased cross-border economic relations.

From the end of the Soviet Union in 1991 until 1995, China met Russia and the three concerned Central Asian states (Kazakhstan, Kyrgyzstan, and Tajikistan) for negotiations to resolve the border disputes. The ex-Soviet states participated in these meetings as one group negotiating with China, and therefore the negotiations in this phase are considered as bilateral instead of multilateral in character.

This design of bilateral negotiations instead of multilateral ones was due to the concerns of the Soviet Union's successor states that an increasingly powerful China would take advantage of the dissolution of the Soviet Union. To increase their bargaining power, Russia and the Central Asian states banded together and acted as one party at the negotiation table.

The subsequent border negotiations were conducted bilaterally between China and the Central Asian states after a general agreement had been reached in this comprehensive framework.

This policy, to resolve border disputes with neighbouring states, was part of the Chinese Communist Party's strategy to maintain stability and thus political power. In the words of M. Taylor Fravel:

> In 1989, the upheaval in Tiananmen Square posed an internal threat to the stability of China's communist regime. This legitimacy crisis, exacerbated by the weakening of other socialist governments worldwide, increased the cost of maintaining territorial disputes with the Soviet Union, Laos, and Vietnam. China offered concessions in these disputes in exchange for cooperation to counter diplomatic isolation and ensure the continuation of Deng Xiaoping's domestic reform agenda. (Fravel 2005, p. 74)

The (bilateral) negotiations led to a resolution of the border disputes, and in April 1996, the heads of states agreed on their meeting in Shanghai to deepen cooperation.

China-Russia

China and Russia share over 4200 kilometres of border. Following the political alienation in the 1950s, mutual suspicions and threat perceptions on both sides of the border heightened. Some disputed border hotspots were heavily militarised. At the end of the 1960s, the Soviet Union had 375,000 soldiers, 1200 aircraft, and 12 medium-range missiles stationed along its border with China, while China had over 1.5 million soldiers stationed at its border with the Soviet Union.

The atmosphere was hostile; the militarily superior Soviet Union (in regard to weapons technology) was afraid of the superior numbers of the People's Liberation Army (PLA). The Soviets feared an invasion of Chinese soldiers into their sparsely populated eastern region, an invasion so huge in numbers that it would be difficult to stop by means of military technology.

And China, on the other side, was afraid of a heavily armed Soviet army equipped with sophisticated weapons technology.

The tensions along the Chinese-Soviet border intensified during the 1960s and escalated in March 1969 when Chinese soldiers attacked Soviet border guards on Damansky Island (Zhenbao Island in Chinese). The precise numbers of killed and wounded soldiers on both sides vary among various sources. The fighting on Damansky Island went on for roughly two weeks, caused several dozen deaths, and resulted in a ceasefire and the status quo ante.

In the same year, another Soviet-Chinese border conflict escalated, this time on the border of China's Xinjiang region to the Soviet Union. The so-called 'Tielieketi Incident' took place in China's Yumin County and what is today the border with Kazakhstan. The fighting quickly ceased and the casualties on both sides were low, but it contributed to the overall tense relationship between China and the Soviet Union back then. (This border conflict was bilaterally resolved in 1999 between China and Kazakhstan.)

The resolution of this border conflict and questions of undeclared demarcations along the Soviet-Chinese borders were critical for the overall development of China-Russia relations after the dissolution of the Soviet

Union. Questions about national sovereignty, and this is at the core of any border dispute, bear a high potential for fierce and protracted conflicts between neighbouring nations.

Discussions to resolve the Sino-Soviet border dispute started in the 1980s before the incidents in Tian'anmen Square. In 1986, the then Soviet President Mikhail Gorbachev announced that the Soviet Union was willing to return to the concept of an early draft (of 1964) to discuss the border disputes. This was one of China's preconditions. It was China's aim to settle all the different territorial disputes in one package deal; after the Tian'anmen incidents, however, China was willing to negotiate separate agreements to reach gradual improvement in the border situation. In April 1991, before the collapse of the Soviet Union, China and the Soviet Union signed a draft agreement which was already agreed on in 1990.

In June 2005, China and Russia resolved all their border disputes. The remaining demarcation issues concerned islands within the Amur and Ussuri Rivers but these disputes represented less than two per cent of the Sino-Russian borders combined. After the resolution of the last demarcation issues, no further border disputes between China and Russia remained.

By now, China and Russia have established 25 crossing points along China's eastern border. Three railway lines and eleven highways cross the border and allow a steady exchange of people and goods.

Besides Russia, China was engaged in border disputes with three Central Asian states, namely Kazakhstan, Kyrgyzstan, and Tajikistan. All three countries are located west of China and share a border with China's Xinjiang region. For China, the resolution of these border disputes was important mainly in regard to security issues. China's policymakers were concerned about the situation in its Xinjiang region, populated mainly by Uyghurs, a Turkic ethnic group mainly practising Sunni Islam. China was on alert because of independent movements in Xinjiang and because of the overall security situation. The bordering Central Asian states Kazakhstan, Kyrgyzstan, and Tajikistan are populated mainly by Muslims and together with the situation of the Taleban in Afghanistan, China feared that anti-China, Islamic terrorists as supporters of an Uyghur revolt might get uncontrolled access into Xinjiang and destabilise the region further. The resolution of the border disputes with the three Central Asian neighbours was therefore more than mere territorial negotiations. For China, it was about establishing a security architecture for its Xinjiang region.

China-Kazakhstan

Kazakhstan was the first Central Asian state which China approached to settle the border disputes, arguably because of its long border with the Chinese province Xinjiang, which caused policymakers in Beijing problems due to the Uyghur separatist movement there. China and Kazakhstan share a border of 1700 kilometres and had been engaged in a short military conflict in 1969 about the demarcation. There are geopolitical reasons why Kazakhstan is a crucial partner for China, because of which China approached Kazakhstan first among the Central Asian states to resolve their border dispute. First of all, Kazakhstan is a resource-rich country with high amounts of natural gas and oil reserves and therefore a possible supplier for the huge energy demands of China's growing economy. Diversification of energy supply became an important goal for China's policymakers and Kazakhstan was an attractive additional supplier for China. Second, and in geopolitical aspects no less important, Kazakhstan is the preferred transit country for China to Russia, and via Russia towards Western Europe. The already established freight railway route from China's Chongqing to Germany's Duisburg, the YuXinOu Railway, passes China's Xinjiang region before entering Kazakhstan from where it continues through Russia, Belarus, and Poland to Germany. Since 2012, a weekly train on the YuXinOu Railway was operated, and in 2014, this was increased to three per week. Now, 30 freight trains arrive every week at Duisburg from China. Duisburg has become the number one destination for Chinese freight trains to Europe; for 80 per cent of the trains Duisburg is their first stop in Europe. And the northern route of the Belt has now become the operational and highly frequented trade route between China and Western Europe.

Before China settled its border dispute with Kazakhstan, it laid the groundwork for a political agreement with economic means. One year before the border dispute was officially resolved and signed, China National Petroleum Corporation and Kazakhstan's KazMunayGas signed an oil deal concerning the joint development of Kazakhstan's then largest oil field in the Caspian Sea. China's initial investment was worth US$1 billion and it included the construction of a 3000 kilometre pipeline from Kazakhstan to China. Later, in 2011, when another huge oil field in Kazakhstan's district of the Caspian Sea was discovered, the Kashagan Field with estimated recoverable reserves of around 13 billion barrels of crude oil, it was again China that bought its stake.

China engaged Kazakhstan in talks shortly after the demise of the Soviet Union and reached several agreements in 1994, 1996, and 1997, which settled the border disputes. Accordingly, China was ready to accept significant concessions, gaining only 22 per cent of the disputed areas. In 1998, Kazakhstan and China finally settled their border disputes after five years of negotiations. And in 2011, China and Kazakhstan established a free trade area at Khorgos to further stimulate trade between the two countries.

The example of the China-Kazakhstan border dispute illustrates how pragmatically China dealt with border disputes in Central Asia—business first, politics later. With this pragmatic approach, China was able to not only solve a protracted border dispute but also gain another valuable energy supplier to diversify its energy imports, an important aspect in terms of energy security. Additionally, China initiated infrastructure projects (an oil pipeline first, a free trade zone later) that would become the forerunner for the New Silk Road project. It has to be noted that China has not always been able to deal with border disputes and questions of sovereignty as coolly as in Central Asia. But in the examples here, and especially in the case of the China-Kazakhstan border dispute, the strategy of seeking a pragmatic solution paid off very well.

China-Kyrgyzstan

China and Kyrgyzstan share a border of roughly 1000 kilometres along China's Xinjiang region. Kyrgyzstan has been part of the traditional Silk Road; today, Muslims constitute over 80 per cent of its population.

The Chinese-Kyrgyz border disputes were resolved by agreements in 1996 and 1999, respectively. China accepted concessions similar to the Chinese-Kazakh border negotiations and received only 32 per cent of the disputed areas. But the first border settlement agreement reached in 1996 included the transfer of 30,000 hectares into Chinese territory. The second border agreement of 1999 included the cession of 90,000 hectares to China. Expectably, both agreements caused vigorous protests from Kyrgyz. The border dispute was finally settled in 2009, in a treaty according to which China ceded the Khan Tengri Peak to Kyrgyzstan and obtained the Uzengi-Kush area.

China-Tajikistan

Discussions on the Chinese-Tajik border disputes were postponed due to the unstable internal political situation in Tajikistan in the late 1990s. In 2002, both sides reached an agreement according to which China accepted concessions similar to the border agreements with Kazakhstan and Kyrgyzstan. For example, China ceded most of its claim in the Pamir Mountains to Tajikistan, a traditional Chinese request in this border dispute. Discussions on solving the border disputes were resumed in 2010 and resulted in the final resolution of the border demarcation in January 2011. As per this agreement, China accepted the transfer of 1000 square kilometres of Tajik territory, only a minor 3.5 percentage of the initial Chinese claim (which was 28,000 square kilometres). Nonetheless, the agreement also triggered protests among Tajik locals due to the general transfer of territory to China and the non-transparent character of the negotiations.

The SCO

The (bilateral) resolution of border disputes was the necessary precondition for deepening relations and the formation of the Shanghai Five, the predecessor of the SCO. In April 1996, China, Russia, Kazakhstan, Kyrgyzstan, and Tajikistan signed the 'Shanghai Agreement on Confidence Building in the Military Field in the Border Area'. This agreement was followed by the signing of the 'Agreement on Mutual Reduction of Military Forces in the Border Areas' in 1997.

These confidence-building agreements restricted the deployment of conventional weapon systems within a demilitarised zone spanning 100 kilometres on each side of their shared borders. Despite local protests against the border agreements, the resolution of border disputes contributed substantially to improved relations among the SCO member states and thus enabled the establishment of the Shanghai Five first and the SCO later.

With the acceptance of Uzbekistan as a full member in 2001, the Shanghai Five was renamed Shanghai Cooperation Organisation and broadened its security focus to the non-traditional threats of terrorism and separatism.

The importance of the resolution of the border disputes between China, Russia, and the Central Asian states was critical for the development of the whole region and cannot be overestimated in its significance for the later efforts to establish a New Silk Road. The mountainous geographic setting of Central Asia make a major infrastructure project like the land route of the 'Belt and Road Initiative' (BRI) impossible if only some transit states refuse their support. And border conflicts, besides their practical problems for establishing border-crossings in the disputed regions, are often a question of national pride. These conflicts, especially when protracted and charged by military fighting, are no longer rationally solvable but become a 'vital interest' to the claimants. The example of the border conflict of Kashmir between India and Pakistan highlights the potential of a border dispute to sour the whole relations between two neighbouring countries and prevent many possible and mutually beneficial cooperation projects for generations.

The emotional aspect of border disputes has to be considered—as mentioned already, border conflicts are often a question of national pride. This aspect often leads to super-elevation of a conflict way above its geopolitical, economic, or whatever other rationally justifiable worth considerations. Against the historical background of the 1990s, China managed the border conflicts with its neighbours well insofar as not acting from a position of strength. The Soviet Union had been only recently dissolved and its successor state Russia as well as the newly independent former Soviet satellites were politically and economically weak players. China could have been tempted to use this window of opportunity, this moment of relative strength in regard to Russia, to press for maximum outcomes and territorial gains. This strategy could have been possibly successful but would have definitively hurt Russian nationalist feelings and created a breeding ground for revisionist counter-movements and possible future conflicts. In a phase of national chaos and international weak standing, China treated Russia as a partner, even offered concessions in the border disputes, and invited Russia to de facto co-chair a regional multilateral group—the later SCO. As a result, China gained much more than some square kilometres of disputed territory. China treated Russia as a respected partner and thus set the groundwork for deepening China-Russia relations in the realms of security cooperation (including acquisition of sophisticated weapon systems and even knowledge transfer), economic cooperation (including the geopolitically difficult subject of pipeline projects for oil and gas supply), and the political sphere (e.g., the UN Security Council).

Likewise, China treated the much smaller Central Asian states with respect in its border negotiations and also offered territorial concessions. In numbers, China received 22 per cent of claimed territory from Kazakhstan, 32 per cent from Kyrgyzstan, and a mere 3.5 per cent from Tajikistan in effect of the negotiations—obviously not the numbers of a rising political, economic, and military superpower that bullies its much smaller and weaker neighbours into unfavourable agreements. Quite contrarily, with these moves, China gained much goodwill and support for its other economic cooperation projects, and eventually for the mega project, the BRI.

* * *

Bibliography

Blank, Stephen J. (2011). Revising the Border: China's Inroads into Tajikistan, China Brief (Vol. XI–14, pp. 11–13). Washington, DC: The Jamestown Foundation.

Chung, Chien-Peng. (2004). Domestic Politics, International Bargaining and China's Territorial Disputes. London + New York: RoutledgeCurzon.

Fravel, M. Taylor. (2005). Regime Insecurity and International Cooperation Explaining China's Compromises in Territorial Disputes International Security, 30(2), 46–83.

CHAPTER 5

Progress of the Shanghai Cooperation Organisation (SCO)

The earlier chapters have briefly outlined the various interests of the Shanghai Cooperation Organisation (SCO) members and focused especially on the role of China. In summary, the members expected an increase in economic and security cooperation to stabilise the region, first and foremost in terms of non-traditional security threats. The analysis of the process (and progress) of the SCO in the realms of political cooperation (and institutionalisation), economic cooperation, and security cooperation is helpful to understand the development of the 'Belt and Road Initiative' (BRI).

Treaties and Agreements

After the establishment of the Shanghai Five in 1996, the member states met at their annual summits at various locations and each year issued a declaration (typically named after the location of the summit, e.g., 'Dushanbe Declaration').

This procedure of annual summits also built the institutional basis for the SCO members' meetings. In the following discussion, the most important declarations and treaties for the SCO are listed. At the inauguration summit on 15 June 2001, the 'Declaration on the Establishment of the Shanghai Cooperation Organisation' and 'The Shanghai Convention on Combating Terrorism, Separatism and Extremism' were signed. The organisation comprised China, Kazakhstan, Kyrgyzstan, Russia, Tajikistan,

T. Pradt, *The Prequel to China's New Silk Road*,
https://doi.org/10.1007/978-981-15-4708-9_5

and Uzbekistan as full members; additionally, India, Iran, Mongolia, and Pakistan received the status of observer states.

It is noteworthy that at the very first official meeting of this newly established regional club the security aspects were already the central issue. Given the problematic history of the relations between the member states, the protracted border conflicts, and the decades of mutual misperceptions or perceptions of potential threats, one would expect that infrastructural and economic issues would be the first areas for deepening cooperation. Following conventional wisdom of international relations theories, political rapprochements and joint political projects are easier to agree on after economic projects between the states have succeeded. As per this logic, the realms of economics (first) and politics (then) precede any progress in the realm of security issues in bilateral and multilateral relations, all the more so when the participating members of this group have a history of conflict and mutual suspicion. However it is the opposite in the case of the SCO. The member states focused first on security issues, more precisely on non-traditional security threats, namely terrorism, separatism, extremism—in Chinese terms better known as the 'three evils'. It is more than a hint for China's leading role in modelling the SCO, assuring it fits into China's regional priority list for Central Asia.

In 2002, the 'Agreement Between the Member States of the Shanghai Cooperation Organization on the Regional Anti-terrorist Structure' and the 'Charter of the Shanghai Cooperation Organization' were signed, both on 7 June.

In the SCO Charter, the structure of SCO institutes and bodies are outlined (Article 4); of special importance in this regard is the establishment of the SCO secretariat and the Regional Counter-Terrorist Structure (better known as Regional Anti-Terrorist Structure—RATS).

The importance of this anti-terror aspect of the SCO is outlined in detail in Chap. 7 of this book ('Security Cooperation among SCO members'). Security-related politics worldwide gained in importance in the aftermaths of terrorist attacks in the US (i.e., 9/11), and security cooperation within the framework of an 'anti-terror' label was generally well perceived back then and did not raise any suspicions. For the members of the SCO it was much easier to cooperate in the realm of non-traditional security threats, focused on anti-terror measures, than establishing a traditional security architecture, not least because of a wary eye of the US in regard to such shifts. But it is nonetheless surprising how quickly this anti-terror aspect of cooperation within the SCO institutionalised, within only one year of coming into being, at the second official meeting and together with the establishment of the secretariat. Common security interests and the high prioritisation of non-traditional security threats were the drivers for the founding of the SCO and its following dynamic progress.

At the summit in 2004, the member states signed 'The Regulations on Observer Status at the Shanghai Cooperation Organization' and the 'Agreement on the Database of the Regional Anti-Terrorist Structure of the Shanghai Cooperation Organization' (24 April).

The regulations on observer status were important because of the interest the development of the SCO had triggered among other regional players (e.g., Iran, India, and Pakistan). At first, there was no need for enlargement of the group and it was not outlined in the initial design of the grouping to grow larger. China and Russia were content with this framework to deepen the bilateral cooperation in various aspects but officially in a multilateral setting (to avoid the impression of a growing China-Russia power block). For this purpose, it was enough that the participating 'Stans' (namely Kazakhstan, Uzbekistan, Tajikistan, and Kyrgyzstan) were included. The further enlargement of the group, especially with such powerful regional players like Iran, India, and Pakistan, would limit China's and Russia's freedom to design the SCO in its sense. And the role of the 'Stans' would further be shrunk by the accession of additional middle powers. Therefore, it took a long time for these observers (namely India and Pakistan) to become member states of the SCO, but the original members addressed this issue early in the history of the SCO.

On 5 June 2005, the SCO issued the 'Concept of Cooperation Between SCO Member States in Combating Terrorism, Separatism and Extremism' and on 16 August 2007 the 'Protocol on Amendments to the Agreement Between Member States of the Shanghai Cooperation Organization on the Regional Anti-Terrorist Structure'.

Again, the anti-terror cooperation within the RATS framework was pushing the members towards closer cooperation and fostered the whole institutionalisation process of the SCO.

In 2007 at the SCO summit in Bishkek, Kyrgyzstan, the SCO members signed the treaty on 'Good Neighbourliness, Friendship and Cooperation' also known as the 'Bishkek Declaration'. With this declaration, the SCO members mutually ensured each other of respect for state sovereignty and territorial integrity (Article 4).

After the establishment of the Shanghai Five (in 1996) and the foundation of its successor, the SCO, in 2001, it took the member states additional six years to reach a declaration about mutually guaranteeing state sovereignty and territorial integrity of the cosignatories. Eleven years after the resolution of border disputes and the following foundation of the Shanghai Five, the participants signed a declaration on such wobbly goals as 'good neighbourliness, friendship and cooperation'. In the meantime, *realpolitik* in regard to such sensible areas as intelligence sharing in security aspects was implemented. The Bishkek Declaration of the SCO is a surprise compared to the development of other multilateral, regional organisations like Association of South East Asian Nations (ASEAN), which first declared cooperation in social and cultural aspects before, vaguely, entering into the economic realm and never reaching progress in thorny security issues (i.e., the situation in the South China Sea).

But besides its lofty title, the 'Bishkek Declaration' contained real progress in respect of the SCO institutionalisation process, again in the area of security-related aspects.

Article 6 contains an important formulation concerning security cooperation:

> In case of a situation threatening its security, a Contracting Party may hold consultations within the Organization with other Contracting Parties to provide an adequate response to the situation that emerged.[1]

This formulation falls short of a security alliance, but demonstrated the growing confidence among the SCO members in regard to security cooperation.

Institutionalisation Process

The predecessor of the SCO, the Shanghai Five, was designed as a forum to facilitate dialogue among countries involved in border conflicts. It was institutionalised only in the form of annual meetings but without any institutional structure or bodies. For example, in 2000 the Shanghai Five defence ministers met for the first time, which developed over time into a regular meeting on an annual basis.

[1] See: 'Treaty on Long-Term Good-Neighbourliness, Friendship and Cooperation Between the Member States of the Shanghai Cooperation Organization', Article 6.

The establishment of the SCO, however, changed this character from a forum into a regional organisation with a secretariat and institutional bodies.

The following analysis of the institutional process therefore only evaluates the period after the establishment of the SCO and not its predecessor, the Shanghai Five.

History of Establishment

At the Shanghai Five's fifth meeting in Dushanbe, Tajikistan, in 2000, Uzbekistan was accepted as an observer at the SCO and the then Chinese President Jiang Zemin (江泽民) suggested institutionalising the forum. In 2001, the SCO was established and comprised six full members, namely China, Russia, Kazakhstan, Kyrgyzstan, Tajikistan, and Uzbekistan.

In May 2003, at the annual SCO meeting, the member states appointed the SCO's first Secretary-General, the Chinese ambassador to Russia Zhang Deguang (张德广), who entered office in January 2004.

The position of the Secretary-General of the SCO is a rotating post. Rashid Alimov, former Minister of Foreign Affairs of Tajikistan, served as the SCO's Secretary-General from 2016 to 2019. On 1 January 2019, Vladimir Norov, a former Minister of Foreign Affairs of Uzbekistan, took office.

The heads of governments and their foreign ministers meet at annual summits. Most observer states also participate in these meetings. Following a proposal by Uzbekistan in 2004, the SCO member states agreed in the 'Tashkent Declaration of Heads of Member States of SCO' to establish regular meetings of the national security secretaries.

Structure and Bodies

The structure of the SCO consists of the institutional bodies (e.g., the anti-terrorist centre), offices (e.g., the secretariat), and dialogue mechanisms (e.g., summits and meetings). In terms of the SCO's organisational performance the secretariat is the most important institution, as issues related to operating procedures, institutional functions, budget, and personnel are all addressed by the SCO's secretariat. The working languages are Russian and Chinese.

Security-related issues, especially non-traditional security concerns, are organised in the Regional Anti-Terrorist Structure (RATS), a body whose establishment was already decided during the 'Shanghai Five existence' (see below).

Permanent meetings, the non-material structure of the SCO, include the following inter-governmental meetings: Heads of State, Heads of Government, Council of Ministers of Foreign Affairs, Conference of Heads of Agencies, and Council of National Coordinators.

The following is an organisational chart of the SCO structure:[2]

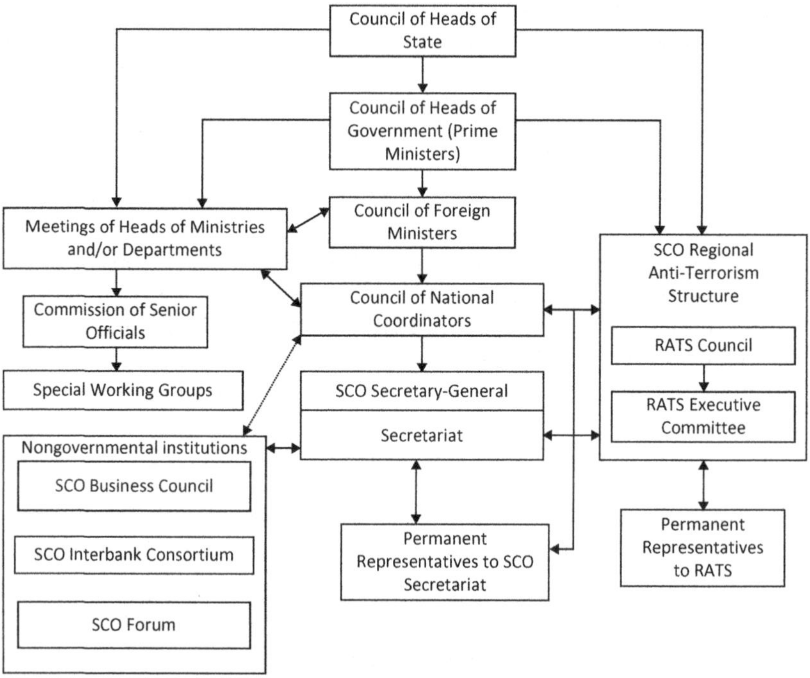

The workflow of the SCO bodies depicted above is as follows:

The Council of Heads of State is the most senior organ within the SCO; it decides the budget of the SCO and meets annually at rotating locations to discuss the topics most relevant to the member states. The Council of Heads of State can delegate important issues directly to the

[2] This organisation chart was taken from the official SCO website but it is not available online any longer; reprinted in: (Aris 2009, p. 475).

Meetings of Heads of Ministries and Departments and the RATS Council for further consideration and evaluation.

Below it, the Council of Heads of Government coordinates economic issues, adopts the budget decisions, and also meets annually.

The Council of Ministers of Foreign Affairs meets annually, a month before the Council of Heads of State meeting, and provides information and topics to discuss for this meeting.

The Council of Ministers and Heads of Agencies coordinates specific issues (e.g., military cooperation, cultural exchange) and delegates these issues to Special Working Groups.

Missing in the chart above is the National Security Council Group, established in 2004, which consists of the heads of national security councils (save China, which is represented by its minister of public security). The National Security Council Group meets annually shortly before the Council of Heads of State meeting to discuss developments in the security realm.

The Council of National Coordinators is headed by the National Coordinator of the current host state of the Council of Heads of State meeting. The Council of National Coordinators meets at least three times annually to organise the nine subject-focused working groups. Input for these meetings reaches the Council of National Coordinator via a chain of command (Council of Heads of State → Council of Heads of Government → Council of Foreign Ministers → Council of National Coordinators).

The nine subject-focused working groups are attended by: heads of border and control organs; general prosecutors; law enforcement bodies; ministers of foreign affairs; ministers of defence; ministers of economic affairs; ministers of transport; ministers of culture; and ministers of emergencies.

These ad-hoc consortiums and annual meetings are supported and complemented by the two permanent SCO bodies, the secretariat and RATS (for more information about RATS, see Chap. 7 of this book). In this regard, the non-governmental bodies which are directly subordinated to the secretariat (i.e., SCO Business Council, SCO Interbank Consortium, and SCO Forum) are of special importance to executing decisions of the senior meetings.

Additionally, in 2006 the SCO members established a mechanism for regular meetings of the presidents of national supreme courts to foster exchange and cooperation. One main subject of this cooperation on the supreme court level was to address cross-border crime investigation.

This institutional structure of offices and meetings allows the SCO member states to regularly exchange important information and delegate orders to specially established working groups. The councils, committees, and working groups reflect the SCO's focus on security-related cooperation and, although to a lesser degree, efforts to improve economic cooperation.

SCO Secretariat

In respect of the representative function of the secretariat, the General Secretary acts as the press officer for the SCO.

The secretariat is not designed to take many decisions but rather to act as a body of administration and bureaucracy. It collects policy proposals from the various working groups and submits them to the senior councils (i.e., Council of Heads of State and Council of Heads of Government) for approval.

The secretariat, in close cooperation with the Council of National Coordinators, functions as the personnel resource base for the SCO's committees and working groups. It prepares drafts, develops suggestions on policy issues, implements resolutions (via affiliated bodies), and exercises the budget supervision for the SCO. Therefore, the secretariat fulfils a crucial function as a hub in the SCO system of intertwined and interacting multilateral committees of different political levels, non-governmental working groups, and the security bodies of the SCO.

Since its foundation in 2001, both the Council of Heads of State and the Council of Heads of Government meet on an annual basis (with the exception of 2002 when no meeting of the Council of Heads of Government took place). These two councils are the highest decision-making bodies of the SCO; hence, besides their importance for the further development of the proper SCO, these annual summits serve as an important platform for bilateral discussions of the participating policymakers. The importance of these annual multilateral summits was further increased by the accession of India and Pakistan as full members in 2017. The high-level character of the SCO summits is illustrated by the participating policymakers: at the Council of Heads of State summits, Xi Jinping (China), Vladimir Putin (Russia), Ram Nath Kovind (India), and Arif Alvi (Pakistan) meet each other, while at the Council of Heads of Government summits Li Keqiang (China), Dmitry Medvedev (Russia), Narendra Modi (India), and Imran Khan (Pakistan) meet annually.

In 2004, the SCO established its secretariat in Beijing, and in the same year, the headquarters for SCO anti-terrorist efforts, labelled the Regional Anti-Terror Structure (RATS), was established in Tashkent, Uzbekistan. The establishment of the RATS headquarters was already envisaged by the then Shanghai Five in 1998. The initial plan was to base RATS in Bishkek, Kyrgyzstan, where the Collective Security Treaty Organization's (CSTO) anti-terrorist headquarters was already located, thus creating a junction for CSTO-SCO anti-terrorism efforts. In 2002, the foreign ministers of the SCO decided to establish RATS in Bishkek, but due to Chinese and Uzbek concerns about a Russian-dominated security approach, the SCO prime ministers decided in 2003 to shift the location of the RATS headquarters to Tashkent instead. In this way, Chinese concerns were reduced and Uzbekistan's growing importance in Central Asia was recognised. Thus, after several years of discussions and a shift from the initially intended location, the project was realised.

In October 2003, the Council of National Coordinators developed the structure of RATS and of a RATS Executive Committee. The first director of the Executive Committee was Vyacheslav T. Kasimov, deputy head of the Uzbek security service.

In the beginning, both the RATS headquarters and the SCO secretariat possessed a permanent staff of 30 employees. The initial funding in 2004 was US$2.6 million for the SCO secretariat and US$3.1 million for RATS. The structure of RATS reflected the multilateral structure of the SCO and in 2004 included seven Chinese and seven Russian employees, six from Kazakhstan, five from Uzbekistan, three from Kyrgyzstan, and two from Tajikistan.

In 2006, the first meeting of the SCO's heads of supreme courts took place in Shanghai. Also, a group of SCO information security experts was established.

Norms and Rule Sets

The overarching code of conduct within the SCO has been the so-called Shanghai Spirit. In the SCO's founding declaration, it is defined as: 'mutual trust, mutual benefit, equality, consultation, respect for multicivilizations, striving for common development'.

Interpreting these values for usage in international relations, one analyst points to the resemblance to China's 'New Security Concept' with 'mutual respect for territorial integrity and sovereignty; mutual non-aggression; non-interference in other's internal affairs' as key pillars. The Shanghai Spirit also resembles China's 'Five Principles of Peaceful Coexistence' in international relations.

Accordingly, it was China which actively pushed forward the formulation of the SCO Charter and China's President Jiang Zemin who announced the definition of the Shanghai Spirit for the first time.

In some respects, especially in regard to the principle of non-interference in domestic affairs, the Shanghai Spirit adheres to the same norms as the 'ASEAN Way'. Another shared norm is the consensus-based decision-making, thus echoing the non-confrontational character of ASEAN relations.

The effect of these sovereignty-respecting norms and the declaration of non-interference is in fact a protection of authoritarian regimes; thus, a non-democratic norm is inherent in the Shanghai Spirit (as is in the ASEAN Way).

The Shanghai Spirit is, therefore, an expression of the mutual interests of its members: stabilising the region via cooperation in addressing regime-endangering forces without interference in other members' internal politics.

Members and Observers

In 2004, the SCO issued the 'Regulations on Observers of the Shanghai Cooperation Organization' and granted the status of observer to Mongolia in the same year and to India, Pakistan, and Iran in 2005. In the same year, the US request for SCO observer membership was rejected. It is noteworthy in this respect that there is no automatism which transforms an observer into a full member and not even a defined process for becoming a full member but only that new members have to be accepted unanimously by all member states. However, the acceptance of new observer states is a decision taken de facto mainly by China and Russia.

Observer states do not possess full participation rights as member states and it was doubtful for a long time whether the SCO would accept any new members in the near future (save Mongolia, which might be a candidate relatively unproblematic to integrate). Indeed, the observer status mainly allows participation in the 'Council of Foreign Ministers' and affiliated non-governmental working groups. Therefore, the status of observer rather describes a privileged partnership than a constrained membership.

The sheer combination of landmass, population, and energy resources of the SCO's member and observer states, however, constitutes the political and security-related potential of this organisation. Observer and member states combined represent half the world's population and resource-rich regions.

In 2008, the SCO introduced the new status of 'dialogue partner' as a restricted form of partnership compared to the observer status.

And at the summit in 2010 in Tashkent, the 'Regulations on the Procedure for Admission of New Members to the SCO' were signed. The Regulations define the conditions for states to join the SCO; however, these conditions de facto erased the opportunity for some possible candidates (e.g., Iran and also the US) to become future members.

The accession of India and Pakistan as full members to the SCO on 9 June 2017 was an important step for the SCO in enlarging its sphere of influence. At the same time, it was a surprising step and might bear some complications. With the acceptance of the two new members, the SCO not only adopts the long-time conflict between the two arch-enemies India and Pakistan—with unforeseeable future conflicts within the framework of the SCO. It also adopts a new set of unresolved border conflicts. Besides the conflict between India and Pakistan about Kashmir, China and India have unresolved disputes about the regions of Aksai Chin and Arunachal Pradesh. Since the resolution of border disputes was a necessary precondition for the successful history of the SCO so far, it is at least surprising that the organisation accepted two new members that are involved in border disputes between themselves as well as with another member state.

Progress and Success of the SCO Institutionalisation

According to experts with access to confidential information, the cooperation between the SCO secretariat and RATS is frayed as national interests of the member states often lead to 'clashes with the SCO Secretariat in the day-to-day affairs of the SCO' (Sheives 2006, p. 2013).

By 2005, the SCO had already identified 127 areas of cooperation but the implementation of these projects was impeded because of national interests. Especially in the realm of economics, the progress attained lags far behind the envisaged and proclaimed ambitions.

On the positive side, the institutionalisation of anti-terrorist efforts can be assessed as successful. At the SCO Summit in 2011 in Astana, Kazakhstan President Nursultan Nazarbayev announced that RATS had prevented over 500 terrorist attacks since its establishment.

The pace of institutionalisation of the SCO is impressing, more so when compared to similar attempts for establishing regional multilateral organisations in Central, Southeast, Northeast, and East Asia.

China's Role in the SCO Institutionalisation Process

The progress of the SCO institutionalisation is both an expression of and an evidence for China's shift in its foreign policy. China's opening towards multilateral diplomacy approaches was realised during the 1990s and one can argue that the SCO was China's 'guinea pig' for regional multilateral organisations. The promising outcome of the Shanghai Five forum led to the establishment of permanent institutions (i.e., secretariat and RATS) and subsequently to increasing institutionalisation of formerly loosely connected committees and working groups.

The success of the SCO and China's efforts to make this success possible (from concessions in border disputes with other SCO members to financial funding and political support) illustrate the new priorities in China's foreign policy. Comparing to China's engagement in other multilateral clubs and on other continents, it is clear that the geographical proximity of the SCO and its importance for China's security and economic projects clearly trumps all other multilateral organisations China participates in. The fact that China's Xinjiang region is at the centre of the SCO (in geographical as well as in economic and security aspects) further contributes to the high valuation the SCO perceives in Beijing.

Security Cooperation

The security cooperation of the SCO members dates back to the time before the establishment of the SCO and even before the founding of its predecessor, the Shanghai Five. But after the resolution of their border disputes (see previous chapter), the SCO member states focused on cooperation in non-traditional security threats, namely terrorism, local insurgencies, and drug trafficking. For China, cooperation with its Central Asian neighbours was meant to maintain stability in its Xinjiang region.

This focus on non-traditional security threats gained further importance because of the spill-over effects of fighting in Afghanistan following the 9/11 terrorist attacks. Besides its importance in national security and regional stability, the anti-terror cooperation was also fostered by (especially Russian) concerns that the US might offer the Central Asian states assistance in anti-terror programmes instead.

Joint military exercises focusing on terrorist threats were often conducted in mountainous areas difficult to access and were comprised of simulations of taking back villages and fighting large-scale insurrections.

SCO as a Means to Exclude the US

The SCO's efforts in the realm of security cooperation and especially the joint military exercises have resulted in suspicions among security analysts in the West. They perceive the SCO as an alliance to counter the US hegemony (in the future), and therefore the SCO has been labelled as 'Anti-NATO' and 'NATO of the East'.

At the SCO summit in the Kazakh capital, Astana, in July 2005, the leaders of the organization suggested that the US-led coalition forces in Afghanistan should announce a timetable for withdrawal and demanded a limit to outside interference in the region's internal affairs.

This perception was supported by the fact that the SCO is the only regional security group without direct participation of the US. The increasing SCO cooperation in the field of anti-terrorism can in this regard be assessed as a response to growing US anti-terror activities in the region.

Pavel Felgenhauer, a Russian security expert and military analyst who works at The Jamestown Foundation, an US think-tank, however, concluded in 2011 that this (Russian) motive had not been realised:

> During the ten years of the SCO, Russia has been unsuccessfully trying to transform it into an "eastern NATO" – a continental military and political alliance aimed primarily to oppose Western (US) influence. Moscow has supported the expansion of the SCO: Iran, India and Pakistan that have observer status in the SCO have applied to become full members. The expansion of the SCO's membership is seen in Moscow as a way to dilute Chinese influence and boost Moscow's role, but the acceptance of new members has been vetoed by Beijing. (Felgenhauer 2011)

But with the eventual acceptance of India and Pakistan in 2017 and under the impression of ongoing and deepening security cooperation (not least in the realm of arms sales among the SCO members) the perception of the SCO as an 'eastern NATO' could have gained new momentum—even more so considering the combined importance of the SCO member states in regard to energy supplies (and its oil-rich observer state Iran).

The US-initiated programmes (e.g., NATO's Partnership for Peace) which reached out for closer cooperation with the Central Asian states have been accepted, despite several setbacks, as a means of balancing Russian and Chinese influence. In the beginning of the new millennium and the inauguration phase of the SCO, this Western alternative has been an important bargaining chip for the Central Asian states to counter Sino-Russian dominance. But in the long term, and in respect of the strategic shift of the US towards the Asia-Pacific region, this option will wane.

> In the twenty years since the Soviet collapse, U.S. policies towards Central Asia can be roughly divided into four phases: too little (1991-2001); too much (2001-2005); a more equitable strategic balance with Russia and China (2005-2009); and inching toward partnership with the SCO (2009-current). (Yu 2013, p. 55)

* * *

Bibliography

Aris, Stephen. 2009. The Shanghai Cooperation Organisation: 'Tackling the Three Evils.' A Regional Response to Non-traditional Security Challenges or an Anti-Western Bloc? Europe-Asia Studies, 61(3), 457–482.

Buszynski, Leszek. 2005. Russia's New Role in Central Asia. Asian Survey, 45(4), 546–565.

Cooley, Alexander. 2012. Great Games, Local Rules: The New Great Power Contest in Central Asia. Oxford: Oxford University Press.

Felgenhauer, Pavel. 2011. SCO Fails To Turn Into an "Eastern NATO", Eurasia Daily Monitor (Vol. VIII–116). Washington, DC: Jamestown Foundation.

Gill, Bates & Oresman, Matthew. 2003. China's New Journey to the West – China's Emergence in Central Asia and Implications for U.S. Interests. Washington, DC: Center for Strategic and International Studies.

Lateigne, Marc. 2006. In Medias Res: The Development of the Shanghai Co-operation Organization as a Security Community. Pacific Affairs, 79(4), 605–622.

Matusov, Artyom. 2007. Energy Cooperation in the SCO: Club or Gathering? China and Eurasia Forum Quarterly, 5(3), 83–99.

Plater-Zyberk, Henry. 2007. Who's Afraid of the SCO?, Central Asian Series (Vol. 07/09). Shrivenham: Defence Academy of the United Kingdom.

Pradt, Tilman. 2011. "China threat" reloaded? China's military modernization and the "China threat"-discussion. Journal of East European and Asian Studies, 2(1), 83–107.

Sheives, Kevin. 2006. China Turns West: Beijing's Contemporary Strategy Towards Central Asia. Pacific Affairs, 79(2), 205–224.

Yu, Bin. 2013. The SCO Ten Years After – In Search of Its Own Identity. In M. Fredholm (Ed.), The Shanghai Cooperation Organization and Eurasian Geopolitics – New Directions, Perspectives, and Challenges (pp. 29–61). Copenhagen: NIAS Press.

CHAPTER 6

Economic Cooperation Among SCO Members

In the case of the Shanghai Cooperation Organisation (SCO), cooperation in the economic realm followed already established security cooperation efforts. It is conventional wisdom that economic cooperation is the initial step in strengthening political relations, which might then lead to cooperation in the security realm. It is therefore noteworthy that the process of the SCO was the reverse. Nonetheless, economic cooperation among the SCO members has increased dramatically since the 1990s and especially since 2000. China's trade with the Central Asian states combined was only US$527 million in 1992 but reached US$30 billion in 2010.

Natural Resources in Central Asia

The Central Asian states and especially Kazakhstan possess substantial amounts of natural resources (i.e., oil and gas) and are therefore an opportunity for China to diversify its energy supplies and reduce its dependence on energy delivery via the Malacca Strait sea lines.

Kazakhstan possesses 68.9 billion barrels of oil reserves and Uzbekistan 4.3 billion barrels. As regards gas reserves, Kazakhstan possesses 5.8 trillion cubic metres and Uzbekistan 3.7 trillion cubic metres. Kyrgyzstan and Tajikistan do not possess proven oil or gas reserves of substantial amount. In all cases, the realised annual production in 2009 was only a fraction of the possible amount. The increasingly important natural

T. Pradt, *The Prequel to China's New Silk Road*,
https://doi.org/10.1007/978-981-15-4708-9_6

resources of 'rare earth metals' are of only little significance for the SCO trade relations. China is the world's number one producer of 'rare earths', followed by the US and India.

The Central Asian SCO members have ratified the Energy Charter Treaty and are participating in the Energy Charter Conference, an approach to integrating the Soviet successor energy supplier and West European costumer markets. Energy cooperation among the SCO members (China is only an observer at the Energy Charter Conference) has to respect the rules set up by the Energy Charter Treaty.

Securing a stable supply of energy, a policy labelled 'Energy Security', has gained paramount importance for many states which lack indigenous natural resources. In the case of China, the guarantee of uninterrupted supply of oil and gas is considered a crucial precondition for sustained economic growth. Some analysts consider disputes over energy supply to be the least negotiable and thus most dangerous casus belli in international relations.

To address this problem and to improve the energy security of its members, the SCO members forced the establishment of an energy cooperation mechanism, a so-called Energy Club. At the annual summit in 2007 in Bishkek, the SCO observer states were invited to participate in the organisation's Energy Club. The main efforts within the envisaged Energy Club would be the establishment of infrastructure, energy transportation network, financing of joint and multilateral energy projects, and cooperation in the technology realm.

Due to the conflicted Sino-Soviet relations during the 1970s and 1980s, cross-border trade relations were disrupted and basic infrastructure was missing. To foster energy cooperation and trade, the construction of railways, highways, transhipment points, and pipelines was required in addition to the opening of borders. The conditions for trade relations were further complicated by dire geographical conditions stretching from mountainous areas to large deserts.

China as the strongest proponent of deepening economic cooperation initiated numerous infrastructure projects in the region.

Infrastructure Projects (SCO as Vehicle for China's Oil Diplomacy)

The rationale for China's energy cooperation with its Central Asian neighbours was again reasoned in China's efforts to stabilise its western region Xinjiang via the declared 'Open up the West' (西 部 大 开 发—Xībù dàkāifā) strategy. As early as 1990, a railway line between Xinjiang's capital Urumqi and Kazakhstan was opened as a first step of the project called 'New Eurasian Land Bridge' to connect China with Europe via Central Asia. Due to the different rail gauges between China and Kazakhstan, transportation remained complicated, and by 2000, 'only four freight trains per day, a local train between Urumqi and the border, and two international passenger trains a week, passed over the line' (Garver 2006).

Moreover, China invested in constructing a network of highways in Xinjiang, and by 1999, five roads connecting Xinjiang with Kazakhstan had been realised. On his first attendance at an SCO summit, the then Chinese President Hu Jintao made a strong push for an early focus on building transportation infrastructure, including a call for a multilateral highway transportation pact.

Accordingly, China was willing to invest more than US$55 billion into infrastructure projects in the region; US$12 billion of this amount was for railway construction projects.

Part of this infrastructure strategy was the opening of the transportation corridor 'Trans-Eurasia Railway' and the 'Uzbekistan-Kyrgyzstan-Xinjiang Highway' built in 1997.

China has increasingly used the SCO as an instrument to gain construction agreements and commitments from its Central Asian neighbours; the SCO has in this way worked as a multilateral facilitator to achieve quick progress as regards regional and transborder infrastructure projects.

China's efforts to improve the transport infrastructure has increased since 2000, major projects being a Turkmenistan-China gas pipeline, a highway connecting Uzbekistan via Kyrgyzstan with China, and the Kazakhstan-China oil pipeline.

China has built the pipeline from Kazakhstan to Xinjiang with a length of 3000 kilometres for US$7 billion. Proposed in 1997, it took several years to realise this project, which was accompanied by the Chinese takeover of PetroKazakhstan, and the pipeline only started operating in 2009.

In 2004, China National Petroleum Corporation (CNPC) and Kazakhstan's state-owned KazMunayGas signed an agreement about the construction of a pipeline connecting central Kazakhstan with China. This pipeline spans from Turkmenistan, Uzbekistan and Kazakhstan to China's Xinjiang region and has a total length of 1833 km. The pipeline was activated in 2009 and envisaged to transport an annual amount of 30 billion to 40 billion cubic metres of natural gas by 2015.

China has played the crucial role of investor in necessary infrastructure projects especially in Kyrgyzstan and Tajikistan, a critical engagement since the states were not able to finance these projects by themselves.

These infrastructure projects are part of China's grand strategy to diversify its sources of energy supply and routes of delivery as well as decrease its dependence on energy sources in the Middle East.

The performance of the regional infrastructure network, however, remains meagre; a European Community (EC) report of 2006 describes some problems that hinder more efficient trade relations:

> In Kazakhstan, for instance, it takes an estimated 93 days to move standard cargo from the factory gate to the nearest export port to fulfil all the customs, administrative and export requirements to load the cargo onto its destination, whilst in Uzbekistan 139 days are needed on average to import a standardised shipment of goods. Moreover, the overlapping trade agreements and rules in the region are confusing, they create opportunities for corruption, and hinder rather than facilitate trade. As a result of all these factors, intra-regional trade has contracted to less than 10% of the total trade of Central Asia, with Russia remaining the region's foremost commercial partner. (EC 2006, p. 13)

In the past, Russian oil was transported to China mainly via railway, an expensive but flexible solution chosen due to the problems of establishing a pipeline connecting Russia with China.

In 2009, however, China and Russia signed a contract about a pipeline delivering oil to China. The China Development Bank lent Russian companies Transneft and Rosneft US$25 billion. In return, Russia confirmed delivery of 300 million tons of oil to China (i.e., 15 million tons annually) between 2011 and 2030.

China's Financial Support for Central Asia

China has supported the Central Asian members of the SCO with financial aid to promote economic development and to improve its opportunities for trade and investment in the region. In 2004, China offered a development loan package of US$900 million to the SCO members. The two beneficiaries of this offer were Tajikistan, which received US$600 million, and Kyrgyzstan, which received US$300 million.

In addition to the offered loans, China provided training for 1500 people from the SCO countries and allocated special funds for this in 2005. In 2009, as a reaction to the emerging financial crisis, China offered a US$10 billion loan to the Central Asian members of the SCO, which was provided via the newly established SCO Development Fund. The first requests from Kazakhstan and Turkmenistan were related to projects within the energy sector. Turkmenistan received a loan of about US$4.1 billion provided through the above-mentioned fund. Kazakhstan received another US$10 billion loan not related to the first one. In total, China supported the SCO members with US$20 billion in loans in 2009 to address the financial crisis. By comparison, China provided the Association of South East Asian Nations (ASEAN) member states a loan of about US$4 billion during 1997–1998. In the case of Kazakhstan, this financial aid was framed as a loan-for-oil deal, while Turkmenistan used the loan to develop a natural gas field.

Economic Cooperation: China-Russia

The important aspects of improving Sino-Russian relations have already been addressed in this study. Following the phase of rapprochement during the 1980s, economic relations improved and also China's purchases of Russian weapons system contributed to the combined trade volume. An important pillar is Russia's supply of oil and gas to China: Russia benefits from diversifying its (mainly Western European) market of consumers and China diversifies its sources of energy supply and decreases its dependency on seaborne oil supply via the Malacca Strait. The mutual interest in energy cooperation was incorporated in other aspects of China-Russia cooperation, for example, loans were related to oil contracts.

Cooperation in the realm of energy security began in a substantial way only in 2006, when Russian President Vladimir Putin and Chinese President Hu Jintao signed a joint declaration on energy cooperation. The various agreements of energy supply included a joint venture of CNPC and the Russian gas monopolist Gazprom, which comprised the construction of a gas pipeline. This agreement initiated the first project of Gazprom delivering natural gas to China via two separate routes.

In 2009, China and Russia agreed on the above-mentioned oil pipeline project, which was financed by the China Development Bank. In return, Russia annually provides China with 15 million metric tons of oil, which amounts to almost 10 per cent of China's annual oil imports.

In the same year, Gazprom and China National Petroleum Corporation (CNPC) reached an agreement worth US$3.5 billion on the delivery of 70 billion cubic metres of natural gas annually to China. This agreement turned China into the biggest purchaser of Russian gas.

Sino-Russian trade relations developed from a low level in the early 1990s and reached an annual amount of about US$4 billion in Russian exports to China and Chinese exports of around US$2 billion to Russia in the late 1990s. It was only after 2001 that Sino-Russian trade relations developed at a rapid pace, resulting in US$30 billion of Chinese exports to Russia and Russian exports to China of about US$20 billion in 2010.[1] The combined Sino-Russian trade volume thus almost met the goal declared in 2004, to raise the bilateral trade to an amount of US$60–80 billion in 2010.

Economic relations and especially the energy cooperation between China and Russia benefit from a bundle of positive preconditions: geographic vicinity; a (newly) strategic partnership; Russia's possession of energy resources and China's growing, energy-demanding industry; and Russia's need for investment and China's foreign exchange reserves.

Economic Cooperation: China-Kazakhstan

Kazakhstan is the economically most potent of the Central Asian SCO members. Sino-Kazakh trade relations have steadily increased and resulted in China surpassing Russia as Kazakhstan's most important trade partner.

In accordance with growing economic cooperation, China has steadily increased its investment activities in Kazakhstan. Starting with annual investments of merely US$90 million in 2000, China invested US$212 million in 2001 and increased its annual investment to US$709 million in 2009. Most of the investment is placed in energy resources, the

[1] All data: United Nations Commodity Trade Statistics Database.

exploration of oil and gas fields, and the establishment of transport infrastructure.[2]

The numbers for Kazakh trade increased from 3.1 billion Tenge in 1993 to 244.4 billion Tenge in 1996. Due to the Asian financial crisis, Kazakh trade remained at this level for the following years, but from 2001 (392.9 billion Tenge) to 2010 (2834 billion Tenge) it grew sevenfold. During the same time, the Kazakh GDP per capita grew from 1796 Tenge (in 1993) to 1,341,955 Tenge (in 2010), a multiplication of 747 times.[3]

In 1997, China (via the CNPC) acquired shares of about 60 per cent of Kazakhstan's Atyubinsk oil field and also of Kazakhstan's biggest oil field at Uzen. Accordingly, CNPC outbid its US opponent Amoco due to the Chinese proposal to construct a pipeline connecting Kazakhstan with Xinjiang. The amount of the two deals combined was US$9.5 billion, including the development of oil and gas fields and the construction of related pipelines.

As regards the other Central Asian members in the SCO, only Kazakhstan was able to increase its production of natural resources significantly. According to the data from the Organisation for Economic Co-operation and Development (OECD) and the International Energy Agency (IEA), Kazakhstan increased its natural gas production from 5.72 billion cubic metres in 1995 to 28.38 billion cubic metres in 2010. Its oil production increased from 423.000 barrels per day in 1995 to 1.64 million barrels per day in 2010. China played an important role in this development as an investor in extracting industries and the consumer market of natural reserves.

Economic Cooperation: China-Kyrgyzstan-Tajikistan-Uzbekistan

Trade volume between China and the Central Asian states Kyrgyzstan, Tajikistan, and Uzbekistan have increased impressively after the demise of the Soviet Union and the normalisation of cross-border relations. China-Tajikistan trade amounted to US$2.75 million in 1992, and reached US$68.93 million in 2004 and US$234.81 million in 2006.

[2] Data of the National Bank of Kazakhstan.

[3] All data of the Asian Development Bank.

Chinese exports to Tajikistan improved from US$2 million in 1992 and under US$10 million in the late 1990s to US$1.38 billion in 2010.[4]

The overall numbers for Tajik trade are 44.8 million Somonis[5] (in 1993), 274.6 million Somonis (in 2001), and 4711.3 million Somonis (in 2010). But since 2001 the two most important destinations for Tajik exports have been Turkey and the Netherlands.[6]

China-Kyrgyzstan trade in the same period was at US$35.84 million in 1992 and increased to US$602 million in 2004 and US$1.644 billion in 2006. In 2010, Kyrgyzstan exported commodities worth about US$28 million to China, while China in the same year exported commodities of about US$4.18 billion to Kyrgyzstan.[7]

However, the most important destinations for Kyrgyz exports continue to be Russia and Kazakhstan, resulting in a huge trade deficit for China.

Overall, Kyrgyz trade grew from 349.9 million Soms[8] (in 1993) to 34.2 billion Soms (in 2010), roughly a tenfold increase. In the same period, the GDP per capita grew from 1185 Soms (1993) to 39,212 Soms (2010).[9]

A huge part of these trade volumes reflect Chinese exports with negative effects on Tajik and Kyrgyz production, which are not able to compete with Chinese producers since Kyrgyzstan and Tajikistan do not possess remarkable amounts of natural resources, explaining their distinctly negative trade balances with China. In this respect, it has to be noted that China has succeeded in maintaining a positive balance of trade with all SCO members including Russia. China-Kazakhstan trade relations, however, reached an almost balanced amount of imports and exports in 2010.

Uzbekistan's potential as an energy supplier is underdeveloped and especially hampered by insufficient transport facilities, similar to its neighbours. Uzbekistan possesses gas resources in particular, and in 2004, China's Sinopec agreed with Uzbekistan's political leaders to further develop gas deposits and to construct transport infrastructure (i.e., a gas pipeline). In this regard, a cooperation of Kazakhstan and Uzbekistan with China is envisaged to realise synergy effects in establishing a network of (oil and gas) pipelines connecting the suppliers with Xinjiang. Since 2002,

[4] Data of UN Comtrade.

[5] Somoni is the national Tajik currency.

[6] All data of the Asian Development Bank.

[7] Data of UN Comtrade.

[8] Som is the national Kyrgyz currency.

[9] All data Asian Development Bank.

China has become Uzbekistan's second biggest customer of exports (after Russia); the volume of exports to China has increased from US$24.9 million (2002) to US$1181 million (2010). The trade deficit is nonetheless growing. China's exports to Kyrgyzstan, Tajikistan, and Uzbekistan have grown gradually, while the trade balances have remained advantageous to China.

Economic Dimensions (and China's FDI)

With respect to the dimensions of the inner SCO trade, the level remained relatively low in the initial phase of the SCO. In 2001, China's exports to Central Asia (i.e., Kazakhstan, Kyrgyzstan, Tajikistan, Turkmenistan, and Uzbekistan) accounted for only 0.31 per cent of China's total exports; Central Asia's combined exports to China accounted for 7.65 per cent.

Later, trade volumes between China and the SCO members increased steadily due to China's interest in energy cooperation, its investment in oil and gas exploration efforts, and its investment in infrastructure, especially transport, projects.

The combined trade between China and Central Asia amounted to US$465 million in 1992. The volume of trade (including barter trade) between China and the Central Asian SCO members improved to about US$23.7 billion in 2009.

It has to be noted that especially for the period of the 1990s, reliable data are hard to access and that 'black market' activities are an important aspect in Sino-Central Asian trade relations, those of which are not included in these statistics.

It seems reasonable to correlate the impressive growth of regional economic cooperation to the efforts of the SCO to increase trade among its members. And although China has invested in infrastructure projects and proposed strong economic cooperation, there are also external economic factors to consider which are unrelated to SCO policies. The main driver of increased economic cooperation was the rise of China's economy, especially after China's accession to the World Trade Organization (WTO) in 2001. Unfortunately, China's accession to the WTO and the foundation of the SCO were realised in the same year, thus causal dependence might be prone to misinterpretation. A comparison of the development of the inner SCO trade with the Sino-US trade volume during the same period of observation (i.e., 1990–2010) is helpful in this respect.[10] It underlines the argument that China's trade relations in general magnified manifold after 2001. In the case of Sino-US trade relations, this effect was obviously not related to the efforts of the SCO to strengthen economic cooperation.

In this regard, an interference is noteworthy, namely the increase of US economic support related to the heightened attention towards the region after 9/11. After the war in Afghanistan, the US became active in supporting the economic development of the Central Asian economies in an attempt to avoid spill-over effects of terrorism from Afghanistan to neighbouring countries. In 2002, the US issued a financial assistance programme worth US$692 million, of which Uzbekistan received the most (US$ 298 million).

But besides this economic support, especially at the beginning of the new millennium, which probably had positive effects on the development of the Central Asian economies, the US is not a major actor in the region (in economic terms). None of the Central Asian states' exports are substantially destined for the US market and US energy companies have not yet succeeded in participating in the energy sector.[11]

In contrast, the infrastructure projects of the SCO were necessary to increase the intra-regional trade, and without China's efforts under the SCO umbrella to establish highways, railroads, pipelines, and electricity networks, the realised growth in economic cooperation would not have been possible.

The Central Asian SCO members' economies therefore benefitted from the economic cooperation fostered through the organisation's efforts. In respect of trade growth and increase of GDP per capita, this development is hardly imaginable isolated from the SCO's impact on economic cooperation. Most investment is related to the exploration and extraction of energy resources; therefore, Kazakhstan, China's biggest trading partner among the Central Asian SCO members, is also a major recipient of Chinese investments in the region.

Kazakhstan's oil exports to China are equivalent to 4 per cent of China's overall oil imports. Combined with Russia's share (6 per cent), the SCO's members as a source of Chinese energy remain subordinate compared to huge oil suppliers such as Saudi Arabia (19 per cent), Angola (17 per cent), and Iran (9 per cent).

[10] Data of the United Nations Commodity Trade Statistics Database (UN Comtrade).

[11] Compare data of the Asia Development Bank.

Central Asia as a source of energy supply is nonetheless an important factor in China's relations with the region. Due to its proximity to China (e.g., diversification of supply routes) and relative political stability compared to oil-delivering regimes in the Middle East and Africa, energy resources originating in Central Asia have increasingly become an alternative in China's energy security policy.

Legal problems (i.e., corruption and missing transparency) 'discourage' many Western companies to increase their investments in the region. China is also handicapped by these practices and unsatisfying legal and security frameworks but seems to be less afraid of doing business anyway. The situation in Kyrgyzstan is especially problematic for investors.

For China's Xinjiang province, the trade with bordering Central Asian states accounted for 50 per cent of its trade income in 2003, and in 2009, 70 per cent of China's trade volume with Kazakhstan was realised in Xinjiang. China's efforts to foster economic activity in Xinjiang by establishing and deepening trade relations with its Central Asian neighbours has, therefore, been successful.

Progress of SCO Economic Cooperation

In May 2002, the Meeting of Ministers of Trade and Economy was established, and together with the Meeting of Ministers of Transport and the Meeting of Ministers of Agriculture, it is the 'main mechanism for coordinating and promoting regional economic cooperation' (Tulibayeva and Sadvokassova 2013).

The Meetings of Ministers are, supported by several working groups, the juncture for implementing policies and resolutions which are decided at summits and meetings on the prime minister level. In close collaboration with the Council of National Coordinators, the Meetings of Ministers (or Meetings of Heads of Ministries) therefore build the institutional engine for (economic) cooperation within the SCO structure.

In October 2002, China hosted a forum on energy cooperation, which was attended by the SCO governmental agencies. At this forum, China's then director of the State Development and Planning Commission proposed three areas to deepen energy cooperation among the SCO members:

(1) speeding up institution building and providing institutional support for energy cooperation;
(2) establishing dialogue and cooperation mechanisms among governments, enterprises and societies and fostering a conducive environment for energy cooperation; and
(3) identifying key areas and key projects to accelerate cooperation.

In 2003, the then Chinese Prime Minister Wen Jiabao proposed the idea of a free trade zone (FTZ) within the SCO. This Chinese initiative, however, experienced substantial reluctance from the other SCO members, who were afraid that China would unduly benefit from such a free trade agreement (FTA) due to its highly competitive economy. As a result, China was intensifying negotiations about small free trade zones (FTZs) on the bilateral level, and in the border region between China and Kazakhstan, several small FTZs have been realised.

In March 2004, four working groups were established to explore further cooperation in the realms of electronic trade, customs, investment, and inspections of goods and unification of standards.

In June 2004, China announced at the annual SCO summit an offer of a total of US$900 million in preferential buyer's credit loans to the SCO member states with a mere two per cent interest. This fund was meant to foster the inner SCO economic cooperation. For this purpose, a fifth working group was established, focusing on transport facilitation.

At the 2004 summit in Tashkent, the member states expressed the importance of maintaining sustained economic growth for stability and security in the region. The issue of maintaining stability threatened by terrorism, separatism, and extremism was also related with the task to strengthen economic growth. Therefore, the summit decided to create the SCO Development Fund and the SCO Business Council. China announced the provision of US$1 billion to further develop trade among the SCO members.

The SCO Development Fund was created as a reaction to the financial crisis and its impact on the SCO projects in Central Asia. This fund was meant to address some of the problems caused by the financial crisis (e.g., depreciation of local currencies, closure of enterprises, resulting unemployment) and was perceived as the first step to an envisioned SCO Bank.

At the 2005 summit in Astana, the 'Action Plan on Fulfilment of the Program of Multilateral Trade and Economic Cooperation between SCO Member States' was released.

The Action Plan, which was finally approved in 2008 by the Council of Heads of Governments, comprises 85 projects and activities. The projects focus especially on trade and investment, finance and taxes, customs procedures, and transport and telecommunication issues aimed at facilitating the inner SCO trade.

As late as 2005, the SCO members signed the 'SCO Agreement on Inter-Bank Cooperation' and the SCO Business Council was established in 2006.

At the summit in 2006 (Shanghai), areas of economic cooperation were further defined and the topics of energy, information technology, and transport were prioritised to be the most important issues. For this purpose, the implementation of a number of pilot projects was proposed and the SCO Inter-Bank Association was agreed upon, which would support these projects as the de facto SCO development bank. In addition, the SCO Business Council was inaugurated in the 2006 summit to further facilitate economic cooperation.

In sum, the SCO summit 2006 was a milestone in institutionalising the efforts of deepening regional economic cooperation, and in the aftermath, trade volumes among SCO members further increased.

Analysts have identified three phases to fostering the economic cooperation among the SCO members:

- The first phase – creating a favourable environment for trade and investment; improving methods of cooperation.
- The second phase – strengthening economic and technological cooperation in the interests of all members.
- The third phase – implementing the long-term movement of goods, capital, and technology. (Tulibayeva and Sadvokassova 2013, p. 255)

The SCO has succeeded in establishing a multi-layered system for economic cooperation, combining multilateral relations with bilateral relations and efforts on the macro level with those on the micro level.

The efforts of China, in particular to foster economic cooperation with its Central Asian neighbours, were supported by a project initiated by the EU and financed by the European Bank for Reconstruction and Development, the World Bank, the Asian Development Bank, and the Islamic Development Bank. The infrastructure project called 'Europe-Caucasus-Asia Transport Corridor Technical Assistance Plan' (known as the 'New Silk Road') was designed to link Europe and Asia to support trade relations bypassing Russia. The project aims to improve trade relations with Europe, but the efforts to establish railways, railroads, and transport infrastructure in the region facilitate China's efforts to strengthen trade with its Central Asian neighbours, too. China's efforts to deepen economic cooperation within the SCO were not undisputed, as Liu Junmei and Zheng Min conclude:

> To financial cooperation among the SCO member states the biggest obstacle is Russia's non-positive attitude. In view of Russia's traditional influence in former Soviet regions and its inertial way of thinking, Russia is likely to resist and negatively respond to China's Central Asia strategy and regional economic cooperation layout, or at least feel some sense of loss and dissatisfaction, which China cannot be too sensitive about, but also should not entirely ignore. Especially, China's ideas about an "SCO free trade zone" are difficult to realize if Russia does not agree to them. (Liu and Zheng 2013, p. 273)

Energy cooperation among the SCO members is an important aspect of economic cooperation in general due to the resource-rich soils of many Central Asian states and their geographical location that is suitable for pipeline projects.

* * *

Bibliography

EC. 2006. Regional Strategy Paper for Assistance to Central Asia for the period 2007–2013. Brussels: European Community.

Fredholm, Michael. 2004. The Great Game in Inner Asia over Two Centuries, Asian Cultures and Modernity Research Report (Vol. 7). Stockholm: Stockholm University.

Garver, J. W. (2006). The Development of China's Overland Transportation Links with Central, South-West and South Asia. The China Quarterly, 185, 1–22.

Liu, J., & Zheng, M. (2013). Financial Cooperation among SCO Member States – Review and Prospects from China's Perspective. In M. Fredholm (Ed.), The Shanghai Cooperation Organization and Eurasian Geopolitics – New Directions, Perspectives, and Challenges (pp. 264–276). Copenhagen: NIAS Press.

Moran, Daniel & Russel, James A. (Eds.). 2009. Energy Security and Global Politics – The Militarization of Resource Management. New York: Routledge.

Petersen, Alexandros & Barysch, Katinka. 2011. Russia, China and the Geopolitics of Energy in Central Asia. London: Centre for European Reform.

Rahimov, Mirzokhid. 2013. The Institutional and Political Transformation of the SCO in the Context of Geopolitical Changes in Central Asia. In Michael Fredholm (Ed.), The Shanghai Cooperation Organization and Eurasian Geopolitics – New Directions, Perspectives, and Challenges (pp. 62–81). Copenhagen: NIAS Press.

Tulibayeva, Z., & Sadvokassova, A. (2013). The SCO and Prospects for Regional Economic Cooperation in Central Asia. In M. Fredholm (Ed.), The Shanghai Cooperation Organization and Eurasian Geopolitics – New Directions, Perspectives, and Challenges (pp. 253–263). Copenhagen: NIAS Press.

CHAPTER 7

Security Cooperation Among SCO Members

The security cooperation between the SCO member states became quickly focused on so-called non-traditional security threats, at least officially. By definition, non-traditional security threats are threats posed by non-state actors, such as terrorism, drug trafficking, piracy, illegal immigration, and other criminal acts. In effect, these non-traditional threats have to be addressed differently than traditional threats, which are traditional military forces of an adversary state actor.

In China, these non-traditional security threats are called the 'three evils': terrorism, ethnic separatism, and religious extremism.

RATS

The Regional Anti-Terrorist Structure (RATS) was established in 2004 (along with the establishment of the SCO secretariat); it is located in Tashkent, Uzbekistan, after its envisaged location in Kyrgyzstan was abandoned due to political reasons. RATS was established in order to collect intelligence concerning non-traditional security threats (i.e., the three evils) and provide this information to the SCO member states; traditional security threats are not addressed by RATS.

The first Executive Committee Director of RATS was General Vyacheslav Kasimov from Uzbekistan. The staff—funded by China and Russia providing 25 per cent each, Kazakhstan 21 per cent, and the

T. Pradt, *The Prequel to China's New Silk Road*,
https://doi.org/10.1007/978-981-15-4708-9_7

remainder by the other SCO members—comprise 30 specialists (seven each from China and Russia, six from Kazakhstan, five from Uzbekistan, three from Kyrgyzstan, and two from Tajikistan) and produce an annual status report.

Furthermore, RATS is intended to develop proposals to fight the three evils, foster cooperation among the SCO members' security institutions, support and prepare joint exercises of the members' armed forces, train anti-terrorist specialists, prepare international legal documents, and maintain stable relations with international organisations in the security realm.

China has been the main proponent of the establishment of RATS due to its focus on non-traditional security threats in Central Asia. The performance of RATS depends substantially on the willingness of the SCO's most important intelligence resources—China and Russia. Despite the improvement of Sino-Russian relations, the sharing of sensible intelligence material is a difficult and confidence-requiring act. This has limited the performance of RATS.

Since RATS is focused on non-traditional security threats and has no jurisdiction to enforce its tasks, it has developed mechanisms to improve communication among the SCO member states and thus supports the national jurisdictional efforts to address these security threats.

The agreement to implement the 'SCO Convention on Counter-Terrorism' in 2009 changed this situation. The convention is a supranational legal framework. It allows the transfer of sentenced persons disregarding the domestic legislation and thus enables RATS to 'supersede domestic legal systems and safeguards' (ICG 2013).

The international non-governmental analyst organisation International Crisis Group evaluated the performance of RATS as follows:

> Its main achievement is development of a database of suspected terrorists, separatists and extremists and their networks and funding sources. All SCO states are invited to share intelligence with it on suspected individuals and organisations. In April 2010, the database included 42 organisations and 1,100 individuals with alleged links to extremism. RATS also compiles blacklists of individuals of concern in SCO countries. Public information is limited, making it difficult to assess and monitor its activities. (ICG 2013, p. 22)

According to an insider, the actors within RATS 'are not a paramilitary, counterintelligence, or intelligence subdivision, but are in some sense an intellectual, information and research staff interacting with the parties' component authorities' (Aris 2009, p. 470).

Bilateral Security Cooperation

In 2002, China and Kyrgyzstan conducted a two-day joint border security exercise, which included the participation of several hundreds of troops. The exercise was designed to address terrorist activities in the region and was noteworthy insofar as it was China's first military exercise with a Central Asian state. The scope of this exercise was small, but it was significant as a visible shift of China's security cooperation paradigms. This Sino-Kazakh joint exercise was the forerunner of the first SCO multilateral military exercise, which also took place in the Chinese-Kazakh border region in the following year.

In 2005, Russia and China conducted joint military exercises for the first time in 40 years. The exercises, designed to improve cooperation efforts to fight the three evils took place in Vladivostok, Russia, and continued at the Chinese Shandong Peninsula. The one-week exercises (August 18–August 25) included 10,000 Chinese military personnel and 1800 Russian soldiers plus 70 navy vessels and over 20 Russian aircraft (including strategic and long-range bombers). The exercises included a simulation of an offshore blockade, amphibious landing, and airborne assault—military operations which were widely associated with traditional security threats and not appropriate to address terrorists. It was argued that the real intended recipient of this 'show of force' was Taiwan's leadership, a demonstration of China's uncompromising stance in respect of independence considerations.

The exercises, labelled 'Peace Mission', were attended by the other SCO members and observer states and set the precedent for following multilateral military exercises under the aegis of the SCO.

In 2006, China and Kazakhstan conducted bilateral anti-terror exercises labelled 'Tien-Shan 2006', which included the border control forces of both countries.

These bilateral military exercises were primarily meant to build confidence between the participants, especially in the newly demarcated and formerly disputed border regions. The other effect of bilateral joint military exercises, even more so when border control forces participated, was to improve the performance of the border forces and thus the border security on both sides. For China, this aspect was important in respect of the border security along its Xinjiang region borders with neighbouring states.

As regards progress in military tactics and especially anti-terror missions, the multilateral joint military exercises were far more enlightening and the SCO members could benefit from Russia's prowess in implementing special military forces.

Multilateral Security Cooperation

The first SCO joint military exercise took place in the Chinese-Kazakh border region (i.e., Kazakhstan and Xinjiang) in August 2003 and was designed to foster anti-terrorist efforts of the SCO members. The exercise labelled 'Cooperation 2003' included over 1000 military personnel from Russia, China, Kazakhstan, Kyrgyzstan, and Tajikistan. The exercise was two-tiered: in the first part, Russia, Kazakhstan, and Kyrgyzstan participated on Kazakh soil; the second part was conducted by the Chinese and Kyrgyz troops in Xinjiang. Nonetheless, this exercise is regarded as the first SCO multilateral joint military exercise and thus a milestone of the SCO's security cooperation efforts.

> In November 2005, a SCO Defense and Security Forum was hosted in Beijing, a 10-day event attended by high-ranking military officers from SCO member states as well as Mongolia, Pakistan, Iran, and India, which by-then already had observer status in the organization. (Chung 2010, p. 56)

In 2006, within the framework of anti-terrorist cooperation and organised by RATS, the SCO members conducted a joint military exercise in Tashkent, Uzbekistan. The exercise simulated an attack of a terrorist organisation (e.g., the Islamic Movement of Uzbekistan (IMU), which is active in this region) on the Institute of Nuclear Physics in Tashkent and included a possible nuclear theft by terrorists. Special forces of all SCO member states participated and simulated classic anti-terrorist scenarios such as freeing hostages and conquering buildings occupied by terrorists. The exercise was attended by the SCO observer states.

In 2007, the SCO members conducted the joint military exercises 'Issyk Kul Anti-Terror 2007' in Kyrgyzstan. All SCO members participated (including Uzbekistan) and the SCO observer states Pakistan, Iran, India, and Mongolia attended the exercises. The joint exercises focused on mountainous warfare operations and hostage release operations.

In August and September 2008, the joint military exercise 'Volgograd Anti-Terror 2008' was conducted. This exercise simulated a terrorist attack on an oil tanker and once again included the participation of the special forces of the SCO members.

The joint anti-terrorist exercises 'Norak Anti-Terror 2009' involved the participation of several hundred special operations forces personnel from all SCO member states (with the notable exception of Uzbekistan). The exercises simulated an infiltration of terrorists on the Afghan-Tajik border and included joint border surveillance efforts and the securing of a chemical plant.

The above-listed joint anti-terrorist exercises were conducted by small groups of the SCO members' special forces and organised by RATS. These exercises were focused on non-traditional security threats (i.e., terrorism) and included quick responses on emergency security situations.

Bigger joint military exercises including traditional army forces, and, thus, normally focusing on traditional security threats (although declared otherwise), were mainly conducted within the framework of the so-called Peace Mission joint military exercises.

In 2015, China conducted together with the other SCO member states the first joint internet anti-terror exercise labelled 'Xiamen 2015'. This exercise was the supplement to the more traditional joint anti-terror exercise 'Counter-Terrorism in Central Asia 2015', which took place in Kyrgyzstan in September 2015. The joint internet anti-terror exercise was focussed on surveillance of websites, forums, and social media. The aim was to foster information and intelligence sharing among the SCO members to address new technological requirements. The exercise was directed by the then SCO RATS Director Zhang Xinfeng and was the first special joint exercise in the realm of cybersecurity since the SCO had established its internet expert group in September 2013.

Peace Mission

After the first so-called Peace Mission military exercise was conducted bilaterally between China and Russia in 2005, the following multilateral joint military exercises took place. Officially, these military exercises were designed to foster cooperation among the SCO members in addressing the three evils of extremism, separatism, and terrorism.

Peace Mission 2007

In 2007, all SCO members participated in joint military exercises labelled 'Peace Mission 2007'. These exercises took place in the Russian Ural Mountains and China's Xinjiang region, for which more than 6000 troops were deployed.

The preparations for the exercises were supervised by the then Chinese President Hu Jintao (胡 锦 涛—Hú Jǐntāo) and China's Defence Minister General Cao Gangchuan (曹刚川—Cáo Gāngchuān) who visited Russia, Kyrgyzstan, and Kazakhstan both in advance and during the exercises. It was due to China's request that the formerly intended size of the exercises and involved troops was substantially aggrandised.

The 4700 Russian and 1700 Chinese troops dominated the exercises and were only marginally supported by the participating special forces of Kazakhstan, Kyrgyzstan, and Tajikistan. The exercises were declared to focus on non-traditional security threats, but urged suspicions because of the employment of long-range assault forces, a means of military power projection. Conducting the joint military exercises in China's Xinjiang region also emphasised China's focus on perceived security threats related to the Uighur separatism movement.

The transportation of Chinese forces was an exercise in itself and a demonstration of China's growing capabilities to deploy forces in distant regions. Most of the People's Liberation Army (PLA) troops were transported to Russia by airplanes, but troops and some military equipment were transported 6000 miles via train because Kazakhstan did not permit Chinese troops to transit through.

Observers from over 80 nations were allowed to participate in the exercises but, most noteworthy, the US was not invited.

Peace Mission 2009

In 2009, the Peace Mission exercises were conducted in Russia's Far East and China's Xinjiang region. The intention of these military exercises were again open for interpretation since 'Peace Mission 2009' was designed as a traditional military exercise and not specially tailored for anti-terrorist purposes.

Peace Mission 2010

In 2010, the exercises were conducted in southern Kazakhstan. Some 5000 troops from the SCO member states (again, with the exception of Uzbekistan) conducted joint military exercises to fight the three evils, over a period of two weeks, 'Peace Mission 2010' was the largest SCO joint military exercise conducted out of Russian or Chinese territory. Analysts assessed the exercises again as focussing on traditional security threats, as Russian Su-24 tactical bombers and Chinese H-6 strategic bombers participated. For China's PLA, the exercises provided another logistic test for its long-range deployability (i.e., power projection capability) since troops, military equipment, and aircraft (fighters and bombers) had to travel a distance of 5000 kilometres. The simulated airstrikes, for example, of Chinese fighters and bombers were conducted via non-stop flights. Starting in the Chinese base at Urumqi and being refuelled mid-air on their flights to Kazakhstan and back, this demonstrated China's growing prowess in executing long-range operations.

Peace Mission 2012

The joint military exercise 'Peace Mission 2012' took place in Tajikistan. Forces from China, Russia, Kazakhstan, Kyrgyzstan, and Tajikistan participated, and the setting was a mountainous terrain in Central Asia. In relation to the past eight Peace Mission military exercises since 2003, the exercise of 2012 was the smallest in respect of the number of participating soldiers.

Peace Mission 2014

Roughly 7000 soldiers participated in 'Peace Mission 2014', making it the largest SCO military exercise so far. With the exception of Uzbekistan, all SCO member states participated in the exercise, which took place in China. The setting was a military simulation of terrorists in control of fighter aircraft and tanks that have taken over a town. Accordingly, over 440 military vehicles were employed during the exercise, including new-type combat forces.

Peace Mission 2016

The military exercise 'Peace Mission 2016' took place in Kyrgyzstan in September 2016. All SCO members again with the exception of Uzbekistan participated, involving 1100 soldiers and other military personnel, of which roughly 500 were Russian and 300 were Chinese soldiers. Also, 300 military vehicles and 40 aircraft were implemented in the anti-terror simulation exercises.

The relatively small number of soldiers participating in this Peace Mission was probably due to the setting in a mountainous area, where small, quick military units are preferable.

Peace Mission 2018

The anti-terrorist military exercise 'Peace Mission 2018' took place in the Russian-Kazakh border region. Approximately 3000 troops participated, of which the majority were Russian (1700) and Chinese (700) soldiers and other military personnel. India and Pakistan participated in the exercise with 200 and 110 special forces soldiers, respectively. Kazakhstan, Kyrgyzstan, and Tajikistan participated only with a small contingent of soldiers or observers.

Over 60 fighter jets and attack helicopters were operated in a simulation in which terrorists had taken control of a village in Central Asia.

These Peace Mission joint military exercises were conducted biennially since 2010, and serve important purposes for the SCO's common security efforts. First, they help training for cooperative anti-threat (i.e., anti-terrorism) purposes, and second, the exercises are demonstrations of the growing military capabilities of the SCO members.

Besides obtaining active cooperation in the realm of countering terrorist, separatist, and extremist threats, the SCO succeeded in maintaining military control within its members' territories. Following a Russian proposal at the SCO summit in 2005 in Astana, Kazakhstan, the SCO members agreed to set a timeline for the end of Western forces' use of military bases.

Russian-Led Military Exercises with Participation of SCO Members

Vostok 2018

The joint military exercise (though mainly conducted and directed by Russia) 'Vostok 2018' was impressive in terms of the implemented weapon systems and personnel. According to Russian sources, a total of 36,000 military vehicles participated and 1000 aircraft and 300,000 troops were included. The high numbers of included material and personnel drew the attention of security analysts and 'Vostok 2018' became quickly labelled as the largest war game since the Cold War. The military exercise took place in the Pacific and comprised navy, army, and air force units.[1]

Tsentr 2019

The military exercise 'Tsentr 2019' mainly took place on the Caspian Sea but the operations spanned into the Arctic area as well; 128,000 soldiers and military personnel, mainly Russian, participated, while the other armies in this exercise were from China, India, Pakistan, Kazakhstan, Uzbekistan, Kyrgyzstan, and Tajikistan. 'Tsentr 2019' was therefore, in respect of the participating countries, a truly SCO joint military exercise.[2]

Conclusion

Joint military exercises of the SCO members, either bilaterally or multilaterally, have always been declared to focus on non-traditional threats and they were not directed at any third country.

Given the dimension of these exercises and the weapon systems deployed, these military exercises have raised suspicions about the underlying intentions of its participants (especially of Russia and China). One military analyst summarises it as follows:

> (…) terrorist movements do not possess conventional land, sea or air forces, nor do they deploy their military power in a symmetric way. Therefore, these exercise objectives had little to do with warfare against terrorism, but were actually nothing other than practice in conventional warfare, employing all Services except for nuclear forces. (de Haas 2005, p. 5)

[1] https://www.forces.net/news/biggest-military-exercise-cold-war-begins-russia
[2] https://www.forces.net/news/exercise-tsentr-2019-starts-russia

SCO Weapon Systems Supply

Russia is the major supplier of weapon systems for the other SCO members and China is by far the biggest customer of Russian weapons technology. The Central Asian states are improving their armed forces' capabilities in accordance with growing economic possibilities, but these purchases remain very low. Military cooperation between China and the Central Asian states has increased but Russia remains the most important partner and offers arms at preferential tariffs via Collective Security Treaty Organization programmes.

China has supported the Central Asian states especially in modernising the border control. It provided Kyrgyzstan with vehicles, communications equipment, and uniforms (free of charge) in 2002 and additional equipment worth US$700,000 in 2008. In 2007, China provided the Turkmen army with a US$3 million loan for military equipment, and Tajikistan received a full military aid amounting to US$15 million in the period of 1993–2008. In 2009, Uzbekistan's border control was equipped with surveillance technology worth US$3.7 million financed by a Chinese grant. The amount of military aid seems marginal but it is helpful to set them in relation with other donors. For example, US military aid to the Central Asian states is US$1.5 million annually.

To illustrate the dimensions of the Central Asian states' military modernisation programmes, some figures for Kazakhstan are provided.

The military budget of Kazakhstan has risen from US$268 million in 1994 to US$1152 million in 2010 to US$1614 million in 2018.[3] This growth of expenditure is in accordance with the Kazakh economic rise; the military budget was virtually constant at 1.1 per cent of the GDP for the period 1993–2010. During this time, Kazakhstan spent a total of only US$893 million for arms acquisitions and the majority (worth US$789 million) was purchased from Russia.[4] The numbers for the other Central Asian states (i.e., Kyrgyzstan, Tajikistan, and Uzbekistan) are substantially smaller, but similar insofar as they solely rely on Russian weapon systems.

[3] In constant US$ of 2017. Source: sipri.org

[4] All data: SIPRI, available at: https://www.sipri.org/databases/ (accessed 2020/01/30).

Progress of SCO Security Cooperation

Following the establishment of the SCO in 2001, the realm of security cooperation experienced the fastest growth of cooperation compared to economic and political institutionalisation.

Initiated by the Sino-Kazakh joint military exercises in 2002 and the first SCO multilateral joint military exercises in 2003, China participated in more than 20 bilateral and multilateral joint military exercises with the other SCO members between 2002 and 2010.

The number of joint military exercises has steadily increased. According to CSIS, a US geopolitical think tank, China participated between 2003 and 2014 in a total of 130 military exercises, with armies from all parts of the world. In 2016 alone, China participated in 124 such exercises. In total, China thus participated in 349 military exercises with 56 countries between 2003 and 2013, the most with the US (132), followed by Russia (120), Pakistan (105), and Thailand (81). But the quality of these joint military exercises and the quality of China's participation differ substantially. In regard to large-scale military exercises such as Peace Mission, Russia is the most important partner for China. In contrast, China has not participated in any combat exercises with the US.[5]

Some analysts overestimate the military significance of the SCO and assess its main function as a 'quasi-military bloc':

> The military exercise between Chinese and Kyrgyz forces in October 2002, and the joint anti-terrorist exercise of SCO militaries, except that of Uzbekistan at the Chinese-Kazakh border in August 2003, effectively began the process of turning the grouping into a quasi-military bloc. (Chung 2010, p. 61)

The SCO security cooperation efforts served, besides practical purposes in addressing non-traditional security threats, the purpose of confidence-building among the SCO member states. Another purpose is to reassure the Central Asian states that China and Russia are willing (and militarily capable) to support the governing regimes and thus decrease the need for cooperation with the US in the security sector.

As regards symbolic value, especially the multilateral military exercises 'Peace Mission' sent strong signals to separatist groups about the SCO

[5] See: https://chinapower.csis.org/china-military-diplomacy/ (accessed 2020/01/30).

members' uncompromising stance. In China's case, these messages were arguably meant for independence movements in Taiwan (ROC) and the Uighur movement in Xinjiang.

Security cooperation of the SCO progressed especially in the realm of anti-terrorist efforts. The establishment of RATS and conducting of joint anti-terrorist exercises are the most visible results of cooperation in this security field. The Peace Mission exercises, although organised under the SCO label, are rather bilateral China-Russia traditional military forces exercises than multilateral SCO security cooperation efforts.

In 2008, the SCO members signed the 'Agreement on the Procedure for Organizing and Conducting Joint Anti-Terrorist Exercises by Member States' and in 2009 the 'Plan of Action of the SCO Member States and the Islamic Republic of Afghanistan on Combating Terrorism, Illicit Drug Trafficking and Organized Crime'. These documents were complemented by 'The Convention on Counter-Terrorism of the SCO', signed in 2009.

In conclusion, the SCO security cooperation succeeded especially in the realm of anti-terrorist (i.e., non-traditional security threats) cooperation. This reflects the members' needs in combating terrorism and separatism movements in the region. Another aspect is that cooperation in non-traditional security efforts raises less suspicion regarding building of anti-Western alliance and is more adaptable to Western (i.e., US and NATO) anti-terrorism efforts in the Central Asian region.

In respect of China's grand strategy to establish an infrastructure and trade route from continent (Europe) to continent (China), this focus on non-traditional security threats makes perfect sense. The state actors along the route have been quickly won for the project with investment programmes and promises of beneficial economic developments and chances of additional market access. The real security threat for China's 'Belt and Road Initiative' was and still is small groups of non-state actors: terrorists, separatist, and extremists. The large and sparsely populated regions of Central Asia through which the land route of the 'Belt and Road Initiative' (BRI) from China to Western Europe passes are difficult to monitor and thus are an easy target for terrorist attacks. To protect the infrastructural lines of the BRI—railways, roads, pipelines—China had to empower the Central Asian states to contribute to higher security. The bilateral military aid China granted several of the 'Stans' and the bilateral military exercises of mainly border control forces were initial steps. With the establishment of RATS within the SCO framework, the security cooperation was elevated to a higher level. The continuous joint military exercises under

Russian leadership, the intelligence sharing among the SCO members, and the supply of Russian weapon systems systematically increased the military capabilities of the Central Asian SCO members and established a security architecture for Central Asia focused solely on non-traditional security threats. This military aid programme for the Central Asian states had been started years in advance of the proclamation of the plans for the BRI but was a necessary precondition for the implementation of ensuing infrastructure projects in the region. The SCO was first security focused and then economy focused—precisely as required for the realisation of China's New Silk Road project, the Belt and Road Initiative.

* * *

Bibliography

Arduino, Alessandro. 2008. China's Private Army – Protecting the New Silk Road. London: Palgrave Macmillan

Aris, Stephen. 2009. The Shanghai Cooperation Organisation: 'Tackling the Three Evils.' A Regional Response to Non-traditional Security Challenges or an Anti-Western Bloc? Europe-Asia Studies, 61(3), 457–482.

Chung, Chien-Peng. 2010. China's Multilateral Cooperation in Asia and the Pacific – Institutionalizing Beijing's "Good Neighbor Policy". London + New York: Routledge.

de Haas, Marcel. 2005. Russian-Chinese Military Exercises and their Wider Perspective: Power Play in Central Asia, Russian Series (Vol. 05/51). Swindon: Defence Academy of the United Kingdom.

ICG. 2013. China's Central Asia Problem, Asia Report (Vol. 244). Bishkek + Beijing + Brussels: International Crisis Group.

CHAPTER 8

Key Players in the Belt and Road Initiative

To understand the success of the 'Belt and Road Initiative' (BRI) (so far), especially the success of the land route, the Belt, one has to understand the success of the Shanghai Cooperation Organisation (SCO). To understand the success of the SCO, one has to understand the interests and motivations of its key players. For this, it is important to bring to mind the situation in the mid-1990s when the Shanghai Five, the predecessor of the SCO, was founded in 1996.

Russia's overarching goals were to regain superpower status, retain its territorial integrity, and, in the meantime, keep the US out of its (former) sphere of control/interest.

China's ruling Communist Party's policymakers are almost obsessed by the fear of losing sovereignty over parts of its territory. This explains China's relentless stance in the territorial disputes of the South China Sea as well as China's rock-solid positions in regard to the sovereignty questions of Taiwan, Tibet, and nowadays Hong Kong. And this logic explains China's rigid stance regarding its Xinjiang autonomous region, which is also central to the development of the Belt on China's territory.

Kazakhstan's ruling class (as well as in the other 'Stans': Uzbekistan, Tajikistan, Kyrgyzstan) is mostly concerned with the prolongation of its dictatorship and to avoid a return of Russian imperialism over it.

The common ground for all these key players to meet up is the fight against terrorism, especially after 9/11, when anti-terror alliances are not suspected as anti-US alliances but instead perceived as partners in the US

T. Pradt, *The Prequel to China's New Silk Road*,
https://doi.org/10.1007/978-981-15-4708-9_8

'Global War on Terrorism'. Beaten by one's own arguments. By focusing on anti-terror cooperation, Russia gets support for its fighting in Chechnya and other troubled regions. China gets its Xinjiang issue addressed. And Kazakhstan (as well as the other 'Stans') gets support to suppress insurgents against its regime (and labels them as terrorists).

China

China's most important goal with the BRI—in economic terms—is to gain safe and steady access to Western Europe's markets. It is no coincidence therefore that efforts were taken to make the railway between China's Chongqing and Germany's Duisburg the first operational connection. This freight railway connection, the Chongqing-Xinjiang-Europe Railway, passes through China's Xinjiang region, Kazakhstan, Russia, Belarus, and Poland. In regard to transit countries, it is the straightest line between China and Western Europe. Compared to more southern alternatives, via Azerbaijan and Turkey, it is more stable in security aspects.

The key players and the most important partner states of China for this route are Kazakhstan and Russia.

Kazakhstan

Kazakhstan possesses a strategically very important position for China due to its geographical location and its natural resources. The combination of these two aspects made Kazakhstan the most important 'Stan' for China.

In addition to this geographical importance for the BRI land route, China and Kazakhstan are connected by rivers. This is an important aspect especially for Kazakhstan, which is located downstream of these rivers. Two main rivers of Kazakhstan come from China's Tian-Shan Mountains and Altay Mountains, namely the Ili and the Irtysh. Water usage is a matter of concern since China has in the mid-1990s increased its extraction from these two rivers—with potentially negative impact for Kazakhstan's agriculture. The Irtysh later flows into Russia, and into the Ob River, making this a multilateral issue between China, Kazakhstan, and Russia. The river aspect is therefore an important point for the China-Kazakhstan relations.

Another important aspect is the issue of border security. China and Kazakhstan share a border of roughly 1600 kilometres along China's Xinjiang region. To secure this border and to prevent support for the

Uyghur separatist groups within Xinjiang is one of China's vital interests and a question of its sovereignty. This aspect alone would have made Kazakhstan a valuable partner for China. Additionally, Kazakhstan is the most important transit land for the BRI in Central Asia. The Chongqing-Duisburg railway connection that links China with Western Europe, YuXinOu Railway (渝新欧铁路), also known as Chongqing-Xinjiang-Europe Railway, passes through Kazakhstan for a long distance. This railway connection has been operational now for several years and the number of freight trains that leave Duisburg or Chongqing on a regular basis has increased steadily. Moreover, this railway connection is the first visible, operational, and significant realisation of the land route of China's twenty-first-century Silk Road (the Belt in the BRI). The symbolical meaning of this railway can therefore not be estimated high enough. It is the proof that China's BRI project will be feasible and is the pilot project for the northern economic corridor.

The Western Europe-Western China Highway also passes through Kazakhstan. This road connects the Chinese port town Lianyungang at the Yellow Sea with the Russian city St. Petersburg at the Baltic Sea, a highway of 8445 kilometres a large part of which is located in Kazakhstan. The Kazakhstan city of Khorgos is developing into an important transit hub since both the YuXinOu Railway and the Western Europe-Western China Highway pass through it.

In regard to Kazakhstan's natural resources, the cooperation with China was initiated in the mid-1990s. In 1997, China's state-owned oil company Chinese National Petroleum Company (CNPC) purchased a 60 per cent share in Kazakhstan's third largest oil field of Aktubinsk. This oil deal was followed quickly by the acquisition of two additional oil fields, and the governments of China and Kazakhstan agreed on the construction of a 1380 kilometre pipeline to transport the oil from the Caspian Sea to Urumqi, capital of China's Xinjiang region.

In 2000, the Kashagan Field was discovered offshore Kazakhstan in the Caspian Sea, which is considered to be one of the world's two biggest oil field discoveries of the past decades. China acquired a stake in this oil field, and when production became operational in 2013, oil from the Kashagan Field was the most important source of supply for the China-Kazakhstan oil pipeline.

* * *

The various interests and mutual dependence between China and Kazakhstan led to a political rapprochement in the mid-1990s, which strengthened in the following years. One important milestone of this deepening relationship was the strategic partnership signed between them on 4 July 2005. China and Kazakhstan agreed to further cooperation in the political, economic, security, and cultural realms and to develop an 'all-round' strategic partnership. The bilateral trade boosted as a result of this strategic partnership.

This included the establishment of the China-Kazakhstan Horgos International Border Cooperation Center, a transnational market place that spans over 3.3 square kilometres in China and over 1.8 square kilometres in Kazakhstan.

Additionally, China and Kazakhstan agreed with their strategic partnership of 2005 to jointly develop transport and infrastructure projects. The Astana-Alamutu Railway and the connection between China's Jinghe-Yining-Horgos Railway and Kazakhstan's Reteken-Horgos Railway were early infrastructure projects between China and Kazakhstan.

Kazakhstan's Multi-vector Diplomacy

Although the relationship between China and Kazakhstan was inspired by mutual interests, Kazakhstan was eager to maintain balanced relations with all three superpowers active in Central Asia, namely China, Russia, and the US.

This foreign policy approach became labelled as Kazakhstan's 'Multi-vector Diplomacy'—an approach to gain the best outcome for Kazakhstan by playing virtuous with the three superpowers' interests.

In the 1990s, as a result of this foreign policy strategy, Kazakhstan was open for closer relations with the NATO despite its membership of the Russian-led Collective Security Treaty Organization (CSTO) and its membership in the Shanghai Five. The challenge for Kazakhstan was to develop stronger relations with the US (especially in the security sector) without upsetting China and Russia too much.

In 1992, Kazakhstan joined the North Atlantic Cooperation Council, and in 1995, it became a member of the 'Partnership for Peace' (PfP) programme. The cooperation continued at a steady level; in 2007, the NATO's 'Defence Education Enhancement Programme' was implemented at Kazakhstan's National Defence University. Since 2014,

Kazakhstan has been participating in the framework of the 'Partnership Interoperability Initiative' in exercises with 24 selected NATO allies.

However, Kazakhstan's relations have sometimes been troubled by other vectors that need watching out for. In 2009, for example, it refused to participate in an important NATO military exercise in Georgia. Georgia was back then heavily conflicted with Russia and Kazakhstan's participation in this manoeuver would have been interpreted as taking sides with the West. Its Defence Minister Daniyal Akhmetov bluntly dismissed the manoeuver: 'We are too busy for that.'

However, in the next year, from 9 to 25 September 2010, Kazakhstan was the host for the SCO military exercise 'Peace Mission'.

The SCO was in general the framework for China-Kazakhstan military cooperation, even more since Kazakhstan relied for military aid on Russia and (via the NATO) the US.

Security cooperation between China and Kazakhstan was thus focused on border security issues and on anti-terror efforts. The SCO's Regional Anti-Terror Structure (RATS) was in this regard especially important for China-Kazakhstan security relations. Kazakhstan increased surveillance on militant Uyghurs based in the country and shared its intelligence insights with China via RATS.

* * *

In regard to military cooperation, Russia is the single most important partner for Kazakhstan. Kazakhstan joined Russia's Collective Rapid Response Force and contributed 4000 troops towards it (while Russia was supplying 10,000 troops of a total of 15,000).

Russia was also crucial for the development of Kazakhstan's armed forces. The Kazakh military is equipped with Russian weapons technology. In exchange for this military development aid, Kazakhstan has agreed to deploy one of its elite forces, the 37th airborne assault brigade, into the CSTO's collective rapid reaction forces. In 2009, Kazakhstan proclaimed that it would acquire sophisticated Russian air-defence systems (the S-300 and S-400 systems). In this regard it is noteworthy that the strong Russian-Kazakh cooperation in the military sector is to a part due to China's role. In the early 2000s, Kazakhstan was eager to acquire decommissioned weapons from China's armed forces. But China made it clear that it would not circumvent nor challenge Russia's role as the weapons supplier for the

Central Asian states. The division of roles was intact: Russia is the military leader in Central Asia while China took the helm in the economic realm.

Overall, Kazakhstan under its President Nursultan Nazarbayev benefitted from its 'multi-vector foreign policy' insofar as it effectively used the memberships in the CSTO, SCO, and NATO to gain the most from the rivalry of the three superpowers behind these organisations.

China-Kazakhstan Transit

The geographical location of Kazakhstan as an important transit route for China to Russia and eventually to Europe is a strong geopolitical asset.

In 2009, Kazakhstan and China agreed on the establishment of a transport corridor to Western Europe and to build a 3000 kilometre highway through Kazakhstan (the Western Europe-Western China Highway).

The Chongqing-Xinjiang-Europe Railway that transits through Kazakhstan was from the start a competitor for Russia's Trans-Siberian Railway, but within the framework of the SCO, the three actors succeeded in managing their interests.

For China, the route via Kazakhstan shortens the distance to Europe by 1000 kilometres compared to the route via Russia's Trans-Siberian Railway. For Kazakhstan, the infrastructure projects not only help to increase its transport connections and thus foster economic development but the country also benefits from transit fees for the cargo travelling through its soil to China or Europe.

China-Kazakhstan Economy

China-Kazakhstan relations are by far the closest of all 'Stans' with China. This is due to China's strategic interests in Kazakhstan. In respect of economic cooperation, Kazakhstan enjoys a unique position, and since 2005, the China-Kazakhstan relationship has officially become a 'strategic partnership'.

In economic terms, the trade volume between China and Kazakhstan represents over two-thirds of all trade between China and Central Asia. Especially between 2002 and 2005, the China-Kazakh trade relations have been more than tripled. In 2017, the trade volume between China and Kazakhstan was over US$11 billion. China is now the top destination for Kazakhstan's exports, followed by Russia as the second most important destination. In regard to Kazakh imports, China is second only to Russia. The trade balance between China and Kazakhstan is virtually balanced.[1]

Contrary to the close bilateral economic cooperation between China and Kazakhstan, within the multilateral setting of the SCO, China's economic cooperation with Kyrgyzstan and Tajikistan is bigger than with Kazakhstan.

China-Kazakhstan Energy

China has invested mainly in Kazakhstan and the Caspian region. Two main energy infrastructure projects in the region are the Kazakhstan-China pipeline (oil) and the Turkmenistan-China pipeline (gas). China has invested over US$16 billion into the Kazakh economy, of which US$9 billion is investment and US$6 billion is acquired assets. Prominently, in 2009 China's state-owned CNPC acquired a stake in Kazakh oil producer MangistauMunaiGas. And in the same year, China bought an 11 per cent share in Kazakh oil producer KazMunayGas EP, one of Kazakhstan's top three oil-producing companies. In 2010, CNPC and KazMunayGas agreed on the construction of the Kazakhstan-China Gas Pipeline.

Energy cooperation is an important aspect that helps understand the China-Kazakhstan relations. China's strategy of buying stakes in Kazakh oil and gas producers is driven by its immense energy demands and its desire to diversify its sources of energy supply. Due to the fact that China is a late arrival at the Kazakh energy market, most stakes of the major Kazakh oil fields have already been sold. But China is innovative in developing isolated oil fields and building a pipeline network that channels into the main China-Kazakhstan pipeline. Its energy investments are politically supported by Kazakhstan, under the requirement that Kazakhstan's state-owned KazMunayGas is a partner in all Chinese investments. Beginning in the mid-1990s, China's energy companies have quickly increased their stakes in the Kazakh energy market, and in 2006, China was already responsible for approximately one-fourth of Kazakh oil production.

While in the past Kazakhstan's energy exports have been mainly shipped via the Caspian Pipeline Consortium to Russia's Black Sea port at Novorossiysk and from there to other destinations worldwide, the China-Kazakhstan pipeline has opened another steady destination for Kazakhstan's energy exports and helped its overall economic development.

[1] https://oec.world/en/profile/country/kaz/#Trade_Balance (accessed: 2020/01/30).

A rather new aspect of China's and Kazakhstan's energy cooperation is the development of renewable energy projects. In 2010, both countries signed a joint memorandum on cooperation in the sector of renewable energy projects. In the same year, Chinese companies started the construction of wind power stations in the Shelek mountain region in Kazakhstan's Almaty region.

China-Kazakh Water Issues

The economic development of China's Xinjiang region is a political priority and shall contribute to the overall pacifying of this troubled region. One aspect of this strategy was the development of agricultural activities. The main focus lies on increasing the cotton production in Xinjiang that already occupied roughly half of its arable land at the end of the 1990s. The increased cotton production is considered necessary to supply China's huge textiles production industry. Another important agricultural asset is the production of wheat to contribute to China's nutrition security in regard to its growing population. But the increased activities in the agricultural sector lead to higher water consumption in the China-Kazakhstan border region.

The agricultural development of China's Xinjiang region into an important place of China's cotton production could thus come at a price for its relations with neighbouring Kazakhstan. Excessive cotton farming is very water consuming—as the notorious example of the dried up Aral Sea has demonstrated.

China's solution to meet the higher water demands for its ambitious agricultural production plans was to increase the amount of water extracted from the Rivers Ili and Irtysh. Already in the 1990s, China announced the construction of the Kara Irtysh-Karamai canal, a project 300 kilometres long and 22 metres wide. The idea was to direct between 10 and 40 per cent of the River Irtysh to Ulungur Lake and by this gain additional hectares of arable land. Additionally, the redirected water could be used for the irrigation of agricultural fields. Another aspect was the transport of this water to the Karamai oil fields to meet the water requirements of oil production. After almost ten years of construction, in 1999 the Kara Irtysh-Karamai canal was completed. Around 800 million cubic meters of water is new annually redirected to Chinese farms and this volume is set to increase further.

The redirection of the river caused problems in Kazakhstan, especially in regard to a Kazakh hydroelectric station downstream the River Ily. A further increase in the extraction of water from the Ily would negatively influence the energy production of this hydroelectric station and thus potentially lead to electricity shortfalls in this region. This would have impacts on Kazakhstan's energy security strategy.

Another aspect of the China-Kazakhstan water issue is the usage of the rivers as transport routes. The River Irtysh is passable between April and October and a main route for Kazakhstan-China trade exchange. In 2019, Kazakhstan announced plans to develop its export route via the Irtysh and the Russian Ob River to connect with the Russian city Omsk and the Trans-Siberian Railway (see next section on Russia as a key Belt player). However, the continued and increasing water redirection from the Irtysh by China during the time of the year that the river is navigable for commercial use could shrink the river and thus ruin its usability as an export route.

But besides the usage as waterway and a source for hydroelectricity, the rivers are also Kazakhstan's water source for agricultural production. The impact of redirection is already real. In 2007, over 15,000 kilometres of arable land in Kazakhstan could not be used due to lack of water. The Irtysh River is the main source of water for 4 million people (of Kazakhstan's total 15 million people).

The problematic aspects of the China-Kazakhstan water issue have been identified for some time and the potentially negative impact on China-Kazakhstan relations as well. The subject was already highlighted when Kazakhstan gained independence in 1991. Back then, in the mid-1990s, Kazakhstan tried to get Russia involved since the water issue would also have an impact on Russia's River Ob (which is downstream of the Irtysh) and the Omsk region in general. But Russia was not interested in getting involved. In 1998, when China's plans to construct the Kara Irtysh-Karamai canal became public and threatened to worsen the diplomatic relations between China and Kazakhstan, the two countries opened negotiations to solve the problem. The talks continued in 1999, 2000, and 2001 and resulted in an agreement for the protection and utilisation of transboundary rivers. The water issue seemed to be addressed and potential conflicts solved. However, the signed agreement did not define any binding rules for the water usage of the Ily and Irtysh but was instead a vague memorandum. China managed to pacify concerns on the Kazakh side without giving in.

Russia-Kazakhstan

The important role Russia plays in the success of the BRI is surely less surprising than the importance of Kazakhstan's role. Nonetheless, Russia is the crucial player besides China for the success of the project.

Besides the sheer size of Russia's territory, its status as a natural resources supplier, its pioneering role in military aspects, and its political importance should not be underestimated. Without Russia's benevolent stance in regard of both the BRI and the SCO, China's vision of a twenty-first-century Silk Road would never have been possible.

Without the acceptance of Russia, a geopolitical project like the BRI would never be feasible in Central Asia, on the soil of the former USSR. Russia might have lost its position as a superpower on par with the US—in respect of its political and economic clout more than in respect of its military capabilities—but its influence is still great. If not in a constructive way, Russia is able to turn developments in a destructive way in line with its interests. The recent examples of Russia's involvement in Afghanistan, Syria, Turkey, and Libya illustrate that political agendas (in these examples of the West) (…) do not succeed against an active confrontational Russian role.

The Russia-Kazakhstan partnerships are based on the shared history of the Soviet Union. For example, Russia's Baikonur Cosmodrome, the world's largest and oldest operational space launch facility, is located in Kazakhstan. Both countries cooperate in the energy sector—some of Russia's most important pipelines for oil and gas deliveries to China transit through Kazakhstan. In return, the new highway from China to Russia's St. Petersburg runs through Kazakhstan. Kazakhstan is considering plans to use the river systems of the Ob and Irtysh to ship cargo to Russia to load the cargo on Russia's Trans-Siberian Railway. Thus, Kazakhstan would gain access to coastal ports, a strategically attractive option for a landlocked country such as Kazakhstan.

Kazakhstan is for many reasons one of the key players for the success of the BRI's land route through Central Asia. Its geographical location is one important aspect, of course, but even in the political and economic realms it plays an important role in the development of Central Asia. Both Russia and China have understood the importance of Kazakhstan for their various projects—foremost the realisation of the BRI—and Kazakhstan has mastered the art of playing an equidistant role between the two major powers.

Xinjiang

The Chinese region Xinjiang in the western part of China is an integral part of China's territory and therefore a special case in regard to the other key Belt players Russia and Kazakhstan, which are external partners for China. But since Xinjiang possesses such a prominent position among China's regions and because it is a crucial region within China for the BRI, it is analysed here as a key player for the success of the BRI.

Xinjiang is the biggest of China's regions. It covers roughly a sixth of China's total territory but is sparsely populated, especially compared to China's densely populated east. Only around a sixtieth of China's total population (approximately 1.75 per cent of China's 1435 billion inhabitants) lives in this region. Xinjiang's geographic location makes it a geopolitical asset—especially for the infrastructure projects related with the BRI—and as a transit region for oil and gas pipelines from Russia and Kazakhstan to regions in eastern China. Additionally, Xinjiang itself is resource-rich; in the Tarim Basin in the northern part of the region significant gas and oil reserves are located. And it is an important location for agricultural cultivation in China but due to its dry climate almost all its arable land is dependent on irrigation, with complicated impacts on China's relations with Kazakhstan as described above in regard to water usage of the Rivers Ily and Irtysh.

The economic development of Xinjiang as a means to counter separatist movements and increase stability in the region dates back to Deng Xiaoping's doctrine of 1979 to develop the economy of ethnic regions and was stimulated again by the 'Great Western Development Strategy' of Jiang Zemin in 1999. This programme pushed several billions of dollars in investments into Xinjiang to foster economic activity.

Besides these aspects that make Xinjiang an important region for China's policymakers, the region is a political top priority due to its Uyghur separatist movements. China's political elite is most suspicious when it comes to separatist movements that threaten the territorial integrity of China. In the case of Xinjiang, the region is strategically so important for China's infrastructure projects that even a destabilisation would threaten the security of important oil and gas pipelines, railways, and highways. A hypothetical independence of Xinjiang would be a decisive blow for China's energy security, nutrition security, and border security—in short, an inacceptable scenario for China's ruling Communist Party.

How real was the perception of separatist option by China's policymakers and the inherent threat to China's stability became obvious when in November 2019 classified government documents concerning China's activities in Xinjiang were leaked to Western journalists.

The documents comprise speeches of China's President Xi Jinping and other senior-level authorities and disclose a system of surveillance and population control in Xinjiang, a system to 're-educate' the Uyghurs and other Turkic peoples in Xinjiang.

The 24 documents leaked, 403 pages in total, shed light on the approach with which China's government tried to suppress the separatist movements in Xinjiang. According to the published documents (which became famous as 'China Cables'), China operated around 1400 re-education camps for Uyghurs in Xinjiang. The camps were secret and were to remain unknown for the Chinese population and global China Watchers. Detainees should stay for a minimum duration of one year but this period could be extended indefinitely.

The documents were made accessible to a wider group of readers by an article in the *New York Times* on 16 November 2019. In regard to the setting of the re-education camps, the article states:

> President Xi Jinping, the party chief, laid the groundwork for the crackdown in a series of speeches delivered in private to officials during and after a visit to Xinjiang in April 2014, just weeks after Uighur militants stabbed more than 150 people at a train station, killing 31. Mr. Xi called for an all-out 'struggle against terrorism, infiltration and separatism' using the 'organs of dictatorship', and showing 'absolutely no mercy'.

Under the impact of a row of terrorist attacks in Britain (mostly knife stabbings), President Xi urged his authorities to value security above individual human rights and to follow the model of the US Global War on Terror after 9/11.

China's policymakers prioritise threats to China's territorial integrity and national sovereignty over other threat perceptions. The so-called 'three evils'—separatism, terrorism, and religious extremism—can in this context all be found in Xinjiang. In addition to the three evils, China's Communist Party uses the expression of 'five poisons' to label threats to the territorial integrity of China. Historically, the five poisons refer to five deadly or poisonous animals one should avoid (i.e., snakes, scorpions, spiders, centipedes, toads). Nowadays, the expression is used by Chinese authorities to refer to Uyghurs, Tibetans, members of Falun Gong, supporters of Taiwanese independence, and members of the Chinese democracy movement.

According to the China Cables, since 2017, China's government authorities have detained several hundreds of thousands Uyghurs and other Muslim minorities in re-education camps in Xinjiang. The documents highlight how alarmed China's policymakers have been from 2017 onwards about the situation in Xinjiang and how threatening the separatist movements were perceived in regard to the stability in the region and the security situation in respect of the infrastructure projects of the BRI.

In a way, Xinjiang is very important for the success of the BRI, as the BRI was built on the concept of developing Xinjiang (and thus fostering stability there).

Bibliography

Kleveman, Lutz. 2004. New Great Game – Blood and Oil in Central Asia. New York + London: Grove Press

CHAPTER 9

Status Quo of the Belt and Road Initiative and Outlook

Six years after China's President Xi Jinping announced the plan of the 'Belt and Road Initiative' (BRI), China's New Silk Road of the twenty-first century has become a steadily developing reality. The first steps have already been realised—the freight train railway that connects China with Germany, the highway from China's coast to St. Petersburg, several oil and gas pipelines from Russia and Kazakhstan to China. The first level is built; the economic corridors will continuously be extended over the coming years and gain new infrastructure arteries. New pipelines will be laid, and new highways and additional railways will be constructed. The already existing infrastructure hubs will further grow and attract additional businesses. The question is no longer whether the BRI will become operational—it already is. The question is no longer when it will be a reality—it already is. The frequency of trade along the existing routes will grow, and with additional railway connections and highways the visibility of the BRI will steadily increase over the next years. We will become constantly aware of this paradigm change.

There will be a sputnik moment in the near future, a milestone event that will bring the reality of the BRI to the consciousness of the wider public—maybe the market entry of a Chinese commercial giant like Alibaba into Western Europe's consumer markets overnight. The groundwork for this watershed moment to come has been done already. The political and security preconditions have been arranged in the 1990s and the following years. Beginning in the 2000s, with increasing Chinese

T. Pradt, *The Prequel to China's New Silk Road*,
https://doi.org/10.1007/978-981-15-4708-9_9

business activities and investments in Central Asia, the first steps for the following infrastructure projects were taken. And after President Xi Jinping's speech in 2013, the BRI really took off.

Infrastructure

YuXinOu

The Chongqing-Xinjiang-Europe Railway or YuXinOu Railway (渝新欧铁路), the freight train route between China's Chongqing and Germany's Duisburg, has become a symbol of the BRI. The realisation of this railway was the first visible success of the BRI, across mountainous and challenging terrain, passing through Kazakhstan, Russia, Belarus, and Poland between China and Germany. For the realisation of this railway and to get YuXinOu operational, not only the logistic questions had to be addressed (such as different track gauges in the railway systems of the transit countries) but the project had to succeed on the political level as well. China managed to literally lay tracks for the BRI and to get the countries of the route at the table.

Since the inauguration of the railway connection in 2012, the frequency of freight trains travelling the railway on a weekly basis has steadily increased. The average 13–16 days taken for the over 11,000 kilometres between Chongqing and Duisburg is lesser than the time a container ship needs for the sea route between China and Western Europe. Currently, the YuXinOu freight railway is mainly used for electronic consumer goods such as laptops and smartphones. But with further development of this route, the number of trains will increase and with it the range of goods travelling this route. However, most important is the symbolic value of YuXinOu. In 2012, the freight train ran on a weekly basis; in 2014, just one year after China's President Xi Jinping proclaimed the New Silk Road project, YuXinOu freight trains left Chongqing three times a week towards Duisburg. The rapid speed of the realisation of the BRI had its visualisation as a running train, shortening the travelling time by half that of a cargo ship on the existing sea route from China to Germany. The BRI had its first visible success and a best case for its capabilities to open new trade routes.

As mentioned earlier, the foundation for this success, however, was laid in advance of President Xi's 2013 speech as were all necessary preconditions for the BRI. An infrastructure project of this scope is not realisable in two years. The timing of Xi's speech and the Chinese use of YuXinOu for PR purposes were nonetheless well done.

Western Europe-Western China Highway

China and Kazakhstan agreed in 2006 to construct the 'Western Europe-Western China Highway'. Work on the ground was initiated in 2008, and after a construction phase of ten years, on 27 September 2018, the highway became operational. Being 8445 kilometres long, the highway connects several cities in China, Kazakhstan, and Russia. It stretches from China's Lianyungang on the Yellow Sea to Russia's St. Petersburg on the Baltic Sea. The travel takes only 10 days compared with the 45 days a sea freight ship needs from Lianyungang to St. Petersburg. Thus, it provides an immense time-saving potential for the cargo along the route in addition to the higher flexibility of cargo trucks compared to the freight trains which are bound to the railway.

The highway is an important addition to the existing railway and increases the connectivity of trade routes in the northern economic corridor between China and Russia through Kazakhstan. For Kazakhstan, the realisation of such a mega infrastructure project together with China highlights its special position among the Central Asia states as the number one transit country of the BRI.

Pipelines

Oil and gas pipelines, especially from Russia and Kazakhstan to China have become critical for China's energy security as alternatives for China's seaborne oil supply. Traditionally, China imported over 80 per cent of its annual oil consumption and the vast majority of these oil imports reached China via oil tankers on the sea route. This led to the strategic 'Malacca Dilemma'. Virtually all of China's seaborne oil supply comes from the Middle East and passes on the sea route through the Strait of Malacca, a narrow stretch of water between Indonesia and Malaysia. China's fear, that in the incident of terrorists' or pirates' attacks on tankers in the Straits the oil supply would be stopped (let alone a blockade of the Strait by the US), led to the development of strategic alternatives.

The construction of oil and gas pipelines through Kazakhstan to China's Xinjiang region became therefore a political priority. Also, the pipelines play an important part in the establishment of the northern land route of the BRI through Central Asia.

Hubs (Khorgos)

Infrastructure hubs and special economic zones along the land route of the BRI play a pivotal role in fostering the economic development along the route and thus, eventually, the trade between the connected countries.

The city of Khorgos is located in the border region between China and Kazakhstan and was developed into a special economic zone. Designed as a dry port, the infrastructure hub at Khorgos is often referred to as a logistic hub with model character for other nodal points along the land routes of the BRI. At Khorgos, the cargo on freight trains from China is loaded on the trains fitting on Kazakh railways. Additionally, it is connected with the new Western Europe-Western China Highway opened in 2018. Thus, Khorgos is the junction between the new railway and the new highway of the BRI. Also, the already existing duty-free shopping area, the International Center for Business Cooperation, will be further expanded.

At the moment, the potential of Khorgos has to be further developed, as should the potential of the BRI in general. Currently, roughly 80 per cent of the cargo travelling through Khorgos is bound for Central Asia instead of the envisaged destination Western Europe. But this might be a snapshot of an infrastructure project under construction.

Besides its indisputable importance for the Central Asian land route of the BRI and as a logistic hub for the freight train railway from China to Europe, Khorgos possesses an additional value as the symbol for the BRI success, a flagship project for a logistic hub along the land routes of the BRI.

Security

Border Security

One of the first steps of their deepening cooperation in general was for the SCO member states to increase the security along its borders. Before the border disputes could be solved, the mutual perception had to been improved, step by step, via confidence-building measures. These measures, joint border control exercises and benevolent signals, set the stage for the subsequent negotiations about the territorial disputes. And with these exchanges and information sharing about the situation along the borders, the first steps for ensuing greater border security were taken. Today, all SCO members benefit from the improved security situation along the borders and this is a necessary requirement for the further development of trade relations in the region. Without security in the border regions, cross-border trade is critically handicapped. Besides proper security, time loss and transit charges—both caused by non-state actors along the route—critically hamper the flow of trade relations. As such, the situation in the mid-1990s was a problematic setting, when China was conflicted in many ways with the other later SCO members (i.e., Russia, Kazakhstan, Kyrgyzstan, and Tajikistan) in regard to border disputes. The resolution of these disputes and the jointly increased security situation in the border regions paved the way for the infrastructure projects of the BRI later.

RATS

The biggest threats to infrastructure lines are non-traditional security threats from non-state actors. The various groups of separatist movements, religious terrorists, and independence parties have a high motivation to harm the government of the country they are active in. Since the government is usually the force that suppresses the violent non-state actors, in the logic of asymmetric warfare any harmful effects for the government are suitable means for the non-state actors. The development of its economy in general and the increase of trade relations with its neighbours are overarching goals for a government, especially in Central Asia, whose states still have to catch up after the breakdown of the Soviet Union. Thus, terrorist attacks on railways, logistic hubs, border control stations, and bridges would be the means of choice. It is therefore consistent, and in retrospect visionary, that the founders of the SCO focused early on security and especially on non-traditional security threats.

Early on, in 2004, the Regional Anti-Terrorist Structure (RATS) was established as a body of the SCO to address non-traditional security threats (especially terrorism and separatism) in the region. Without this focus on security cooperation, the intelligence sharing among the SCO members, and the sometimes harsh procedures against suspected terrorists, the security situation in Central Asia would be fundamentally less stable. Pipelines, railways, and bridges would be preferred targets of terrorist to damage the national infrastructure, harm the government, and create an atmosphere of chaos—a catastrophic scenario for such a huge infrastructure project as the BRI, spanning over the continents Europe, Africa, and Asia. For the situation in Central Asia, with focus on the pipelines, railways, and highways, the security cooperation among the SCO members and the establishment of RATS was crucial for the successful realisation of the BRI.

Peace Mission

Peace Mission was both a confidence-building measure for the SCO members—especially for China and Russia as a means to strengthen their military alliance—and an important factor in building a security architecture for Central Asia. The multilateral military exercises, held on a biennial basis, were private lessons of Russian military tactics for the other SCO members (China expressly included). By demonstrating its military capabilities and superiority in regard to its SCO peers, Russia could manifest its position as the military leader in the region, a position accepted and not challenged by China, which was eager to benefit from the deepening military cooperation with Russia. The periodic demonstration of its superior military capabilities, a show of force in a collegial setting, established the SCO hierarchy in respect of military matters. Last but not least, the Peace Mission exercises were a roadshow for Russian weapons systems, which could be exported to the other SCO members. The proliferation of Russian weapons systems in Central Asia secured Russia its position as the supplier (and in regard to maintenance contracts). Additionally, the use of Russian military technology among the SCO members increased the interoperability of forces.

The Peace Mission military exercises were much more than merely joint military exercises. They were an important means for the establishment of a Central Asian security architecture with Russia on top. They helped and still help the SCO member states' armies to improve their performance and thus increase the security situation in the region. Additionally, the joint military exercises are a means of transparency and permanent confidence-building measure.

Bilateral Exercises

Parallel to the huge multilateral military exercises of Peace Mission, smaller bilateral military exercises between two SCO members helped to decrease mistrust and to foster (cross-border) security cooperation. Before China and Russia engaged in Peace Mission, they conducted bilateral military exercises. In 1999, China's Navy (PLAN) and Russia's Pacific Fleet held naval exercises in the East China Sea. And in 2001, the two armies conducted bilateral military exercises with strategic bombers before the first Peace Mission military exercise was organised in 2005.

China continually holds military exercises with the Central Asian states (the 'Stans'), much smaller in scope but helpful to maintain trustful relations with other forces over the borders. Similarly, since 2003 China has been engaged in military exercises with Pakistan on an annual basis. And in 2014, China conducted its first military exercises with Iran. Both Iran and Pakistan are important partners for the southern land route of the BRI and for the maritime route (the Road).

Russian Weapons Supply

Russia's supply of weapon systems for the SCO member states has been fundamental for the building up and modernisation of their armies. Russia's policy for weapons systems exports was less restrictive and non-conditional than that of US and European weapons exporters. And Russia's weapons systems were cheaper, especially the used ones.

In the 1990s and early 2000s, the financially weak Central Asian states relied on the supply of affordable Russian weapons technology to build their national armies. Subsequently, the usage of Russian weapons became logical since Russia took the helm in the military affairs within the SCO and the usage of Russian systems among the SCO members increased the interoperability of the forces as stated above.

Outlook

The US Response to the BRI

In 2019, the US Overseas Private Investment Cooperation (OPIC) founded together with Australia's Department of Foreign Affairs and the Japan Bank for International Cooperation a joint initiative labelled 'Blue Dot Network'. The initiative is designed as a forum, a facilitator for global infrastructure projects, and brings together government bodies and private investors. The geographical focus of the Blue Dot Network is initially the Indo-Pacific region but is not limited to it. In effect, infrastructure projects around the world are on the agenda of this group.

The US OPIC was founded in 1971 to support US businesses to invest in emerging markets. The services provided span from risk management tools and networking with investors to political support in emerging countries. In its own words:

> OPIC helps American businesses gain footholds in new markets, catalyzes new revenues and contributes to jobs and growth opportunities both at home and abroad. OPIC fulfills its mission by providing businesses with financing, political risk insurance, advocacy and by partnering with private equity fund managers.[1]

In 2019, OPIC passed the milestone of investing US$100 billion in development projects since its foundation in 1971. From 1 January 2020 onwards, the group was renamed U.S. International Development Finance Corporation (DFC) and virtually became the US development bank. The goals remain the same, providing support for US companies to invest in emerging countries and reinforcing US foreign policy and national security interests. Pushed by US President Donald Trump and the 'Better Utilization of Investments Leading to Development' (BUILD) Act, DFC is equipped with an investment limit of US$60 billion, more than double OPIC's limit. The investment focus is on the energy sector, healthcare, critical infrastructure, and technology projects.[2]

Contrary to China's approach to finance and in realising infrastructure projects along the BRI routes mainly by itself, the Blue Dot Network is, at least in this early stages, designed as a rating system for infrastructure: roads, railways, ports, bridges. It partners the US, Japan, and Australia and will provide technical support for infrastructure projects, facilitate investments, and foster transparency.

To this day, it remains vague as to what exactly the trilateral project Blue Dot Network is designed for. But since it is driven by the US and since US President Trump is the proponent and initiator of an emerging tariff war to contain China's economic growth—and since the two partners Australia and Japan are the most important allies of the US in the region—it is fair to assume that the Blue Dot Network was created as an

[1] OPIC Press Release, December 6, 2019 – https://www.dfc.gov/media/opic-press-releases/opic-surpasses-100-billion-historical-commitments-during-milestone-year

[2] DFC Press Release, January 2, 2020 – https://www.dfc.gov/media/press-releases/us-international-development-finance-corporation-begins-operations

alternative model for China's so-far unchallenged growing economic access to Asia and Central Asia.

Southern Economic Corridor (Iran-Turkey)

The Southern land route of the BRI from China to Western Europe travels from China through Central Asia and then via Iran and Turkey to Eastern Europe (Bulgaria) and finally to Western Europe. The potential of this route, for railways, highways, and pipelines, is at least as promising as the northern land route through Kazakhstan and Russia. Additionally, this land route possesses further opportunities for linking several routes if connected by railway with the port of Gwadar in Pakistan.

Maritime Route (Road): 'String of Pearls'

Beginning at the turn of the millennium, China started to develop port facilities for replenishment purposes and as logistic hubs along the sea lanes in the Indian Ocean. Over the past years, China has thus either initiated port modernisation or established completely new port facilities in Myanmar (Hianggyi, Akyab, Mergui), Bangladesh (Chittagong), Pakistan (Gwadar), and Sri Lanka (Hambantota). This row of ports has been phrased as 'China's String of Pearls' and has raised some eyebrows of geostrategic analysts wondering about China's ambitions in the Indian Ocean. Less surprisingly, it is entirely defensive in Beijing's point of view.

Additionally, China is about to establish a series of port partnerships in littoral states along the sea lanes connecting Africa and the Middle East with Northeast Asia. The pearls in this String of Pearls are harbours located in Sri Lanka, Pakistan, Bangladesh, Burma, and China's Sanya base on Hainan. These ports (except Sanya) are not military in nature but are qualified as improving China's power projection capabilities through supply options, thus raising worries in states like India, which feel increasingly encircled and fear that these initiatives might translate into strategic partnerships.[3]

[3] See Pradt (2016): "China's New Foreign Policy".

Maritime Route: Arctic

A future sea route from China to Western Europe might be a sea lane along the Russian Arctic coast called the Northern Sea Route. Being difficult to navigate since parts of this sea lane are free of ice for only two months in a year, this sea lane might become more accessible as a result of the global climate warming. In the past, a convoying icebreaker was mandatory for ships passing the Northern Sea Route. But in 2017, the first ship passed this route without the use of icebreakers. And in 2018, a new ship class of cargo ships with icebreaker capabilities was introduced that potentially could be implemented on the Northern Sea Route.

However, despite the climate change's impact on the Arctic in general and the Northern Sea Route in particular, experts predict that it will take several decades before cargo ships between China and Europe will be able to shortcut the distance through the Arctic.

Closing Remarks

China's work to realise the Belt and Road Initiative (BRI) had begun even before President Xi Jinping proclaimed the project in 2013. Indeed, one crucial link for the land route through Central Asia, the YuXinOu Railway from China to Germany, was already operational in 2012. But the preliminary work took place even earlier, long before the project was precisely planned and named 'One Belt, One Road' (OBOR), and later the BRI.

When Chinese policymakers assessed the situation in Central Asia, the immediate necessity to increase security in general and border security in particular was obvious. To create stability in the region in a long-term perspective, the improvement of the economic performance of the 'Stans' was mandatory to curb separatist and political extremist movements. Political stability through economic development was the objective. The two aspects of security and economic development are directly interdependent—in the future the two will require and support each other and will only thrive together.

This is when the Shanghai Cooperation Organisation (SCO) entered the stage, the multilateral club of China, Russia, and the 'Stans' Kazakhstan, Uzbekistan, Tajikistan, and Kyrgyzstan. The SCO provided its members with a framework to develop its conventional armies to address especially non-traditional security threats such as terrorism, trafficking, and political insurgents. The SCO became insofar the guarantor of security in Central Asia—a precondition for the later realisation of the BRI. Through cooperation in the security sector (and the resolution of border disputes, a precondition for the establishment of the SCO), the SCO members also deepened cooperation in the political and economic realms. Thus, at the beginning of the new millennium, the stage was set for further development of trade and economic exchange between China, Russia, and the Central Asian states. But what was lacking was a sound infrastructure network to connect the resource-rich regions with the industrial regions and the producing regions with additional consumer markets.

Around this time, the potential of a grand infrastructure project became clearer and the first links—pipelines, railways, and roads—were realised. But it still lacked the vision for a grand strategy in a geopolitical sense. It was only in 2013, when Xi Jinping announced his plans to create a twenty-first century New Silk Road, that a modern vision of a land route for trade between China and Western Europe developed—the plan to directly link the world's workbench (China) with the world's biggest consumer market (Europe), with the resource-rich Central Asia and Russia in the middle and the energy-hungry European states and China to the left and the right. And the idea that a connection of all these different parts of the puzzle would foster the general economic development of many regions emerged.

For the realisation of this grand infrastructure project, China has so far taken immense efforts, starting with the conceding stance in border disputes in the 1990s to set the stage for the later SCO. Subsequently, China has been supportive with knowledge and loans to realise infrastructure projects in Central Asia (not to its economic disadvantage). And it has been an active investor in Central Asia, especially in the energy sector (again, not to its disadvantage). However, for the realisation of the BRI, and that is the focus of this book, China's role in Central Asia was continuously results-driven.

China quickly identified Russia as a key player for stabilising Central Asia, since against the interests of Russia, no lasting political or security stability in the region would be possible. Moreover, Russia as a provider of both natural resources and weapons technology was pivotal for the continuous rise of China in the economic and security realms. The de facto alliance of the two permanent members in the United Nations Security Council was therefore only a logical move. China and Russia cultivated their partnership over the past three decades and jointly lead the SCO as the multilateral political entity and security architect for Central Asia, and developed it into the new energy club of our time.

The other key player for the BRI land route so far has been Kazakhstan. China became early in the 1990s an investor in Kazakh oil companies (and thus a stakeholder of Kazakh oil fields). Oil and gas pipelines from Kazakh sources as well as from Russian fields run through Kazakhstan. Additionally, the first freight railway from China to Western Europe and the newly finalised highway from China to St. Petersburg pass through Kazakhstan. And the currently largest logistic hub with model character for other junctions in Central Asia is located in Khorgos at the border between China and Kazakhstan. Finally, Kazakhstan shares an almost 1800 kilometre long border with China, more precisely with China's Xinjiang region. Given the unstable political situation in Xinjiang, it was a priority for China to improve relations with Kazakhstan and to increase border security on both sides of the border, to prevent separatists, terrorists, and extremists from entering Xinjiang.

As a result, the partnership with Kazakhstan was beneficial for China in various aspects, and for the realisation of the BRI, so far, Kazakhstan has played a central role.

The manufacturer's authorised representative in the EU is Springer Nature Customer Service Centre GmbH, Europaplatz 3, 69115 Heidelberg, Germany. If you have any concerns regarding our products, please contact ProductSafety@springernature.com

Printed and bound by CPI Group (UK) Ltd, Croydon, CR0 4YY
30/09/2026
02225514-0006